Contents

The views expressed in this publication are not necessarily those of the Royal Agricultural Society of England.

Preface

Organic farming is a contentious subject. It is growing fast with strong support, but there are many voices that query its long-term value. One cannot judge organic farming on its own; it must be seen in comparison with the alternatives, the most important of which is conventional farming. However, a number of other variants are developing rapidly, based around Integrated Farm Management techniques.

These are important issues. Conventional farming has often been criticised on environmental grounds and the use of the farmland of Britain is a major issue at present. All members of the farming population, now and in the future, will be affected. This whole subject is therefore of major interest to the Royal Agricultural Society of England, which has managed and organised the production of this publication. These matters are also of great interest to the Fertiliser Manufacturers' Association and the Crop Protection Association and they have therefore given support to the Royal Agricultural Society of England to enable this work to proceed.

The society acknowledges the wide variety of opinions and the intense debate within British farming on these issues. It was felt that the majority of the literature on the subject was written from a strongly committed point of view. As a consequence a group of authors has been selected with a wide experience of the relevant fields in an attempt to provide an unbiased, scientific study of this area. The panel does not have strong prior connections with any one farming system and is so multidisciplinary that few of the members have worked together previously. All have been guaranteed complete independence.

Mike Calvert, Royal Agricultural Society of England
November 2000

Shades of Green -

A review of UK farming systems

ii

First Published in 2000 by
Royal Agricultural Society of England
National Agricultural Centre
Stoneleigh Park
Warwickshire CV8 2LZ

ISBN 0 902629 99 9

Printed in Great Britain by Page Bros Ltd
Norwich

Chapter One

Introduction

Dr P B Tinker OBE, MA, PhD, DSc, FIBiol, FRSC, FRAgS

1.1. Historical background

1.1.1. The origins of farming

Ever since arable agriculture was developed different farming systems have been used. In the river valleys, soil fertility depended greatly upon the annual flood and the silt deposited. Elsewhere, systems that depended much more on nutrient cycling were developed. The Romans used organic manures, green manures, liming, fallows, rotations and mixed farming with leys (Fussell, 1972) in a way that has obvious parallels with modern organic farming. This classical system was further modified in the Agricultural Revolution of the 18th Century that produced the Norfolk 4-course rotation and similar systems. The main constraints on productivity were shortages of the essential nutrient elements in the soil, pests and diseases.

The first step in the development of scientific agriculture was the invention of artificial fertilisers around 1850. Even then these aroused opposition, and the long-term experiments with chemical fertilisers at Rothamsted Experimental Station were started to determine if these damaged the soil properties and crop yields over long periods (see Greenland, this volume). This argument had links with the rather earlier controversy about 'vital force', that claimed there was a truly fundamental difference between organic compounds (e.g. manures) and inorganic compounds (e.g. fertilizers).

1.1.2. The modern period

From the late nineteenth century onwards crop protection developed, and various simple biocides were used, such as arsenic and copper compounds. Later more complex materials such as the organophosphates were invented. The rates of fertilizer used increased slowly. Plant breeding became more scientific, (though simple breeding must have been in progress for millennia), and the newer cultivars were more responsive to fertilisers. A generalised suspicion of new methods and chemical fertilisers continued, and Daniel Hall (1941 p.262) complained that "....we are being asked to resuscitate the farming of the earlier half of the nineteenth century".

In the post-war period the use of fertiliser and crop protection chemicals increased sharply in the developed countries, together with the production of new and much improved cultivars, and with full mechanisation (Cooke, 1967). Quite astonishing increases in yield were obtained during this period, thereby preventing widespread food shortages. The same changes reached many tropical countries later in the Green Revolution, though there are still many subsistence farmers who use virtually no modern methods because they cannot afford bought inputs.

During this period evidence appeared that the modern methods could carry dangers with them. Organic manures and leys can raise the organic matter status of soils, and in some cases their absence caused soil structural problems (Greenland, this volume). Excessive use of crop protection chemicals could damage wild-life (Carson, 1972; see Greenwood, this volume). Other changes during this intensification also caused criticism. Hedges and field boundaries were often removed to make cultivation with large machinery easier, and this caused damage to wildlife and to the rural landscape (Shoard, 1980). Briefly, the new intensive farming was blamed for (1) damage to soil structure and quality, (2) damage to the environment, water, wildlife and landscape, (3) health hazards in food, (4) reduction of food quality (5) energy-wastage (6) ethically unacceptable animal production systems (7) economic loss to farmers and society. Similar or worse problems appeared in some tropical countries when intensive methods were adopted there (Tinker, 1997). The use of genetic manipulation and biotechnology to produce more efficient crops in the past few years has caused more major objections, but there is no space to deal with this specialised subject in this publication.

1.2. Farming systems

1.2.1. Organic, integrated and conventional agriculture

There are many ways of classifying farming systems, such as mixed farming, hill farming, etc. In this book we focus on the three types in the heading. There are many variants, but the principles underlying these farming systems are general. Organic agriculture is certainly the most closely defined of the three systems discussed in this book, and this precision is a considerable advantage to the organic movement.

1.2.2. Intensive (conventional) agriculture

Of course 'conventional' agriculture is not a single farming system, but effectively includes all mainstream agriculture in developed countries at present. The main drive is towards productivity and efficiency, as in most industry and commerce. The lower prices for agricultural products in recent years, and the demands for "cheap food" have encouraged this attitude.

Conventional agriculture covers a wide range of practices. For example, it is perfectly possible to use agrochemicals and fertilisers as recommended, but also to maintain wide hedges, conservation margins and other features of environment-friendly farming, together with strict standards of animal welfare. In this book, we take conventional agriculture in the UK to include all treatments as specified by ADAS, or by the manufacturers of chemicals sold for agricultural use (agricultural chemicals are controlled by MAFF through a list of acceptable materials and methods for their use and disposal). The objective is to apply just sufficient chemical to produce a yield response up to the point where further application would on average cost more than the gain in additional product. However, this point is often difficult to determine, and there is little doubt that many farmers exceed or (more rarely) undershoot the proper rate, or apply it incorrectly. This is unavoidable in any agricultural system, but is undesirable and should be controlled as far as possible.

This conventional approach implies using science and technology to its fullest extent. It permits the use of any chemical found to be beneficial and without serious disadvantages, and this is probably the sharpest point of difference with organic farming. The technologies, the chemicals and their potential for damage to the countryside or the consumer vary widely. Where significant damage has been proven in the past scientific research has so far always found alternative methods that are safer, but still effective. Regulation of the uses of chemicals has increased rapidly and has proved to be effective when applied in a determined fashion. The safety of all forms of agriculture now depends upon careful regulation by the authorities, and stringent scientific tests for possible causes of damage or danger. Nevertheless, recent disasters such as the BSE crisis in stock farming (that in origin apparently had nothing to do with synthetic chemicals, as far as is known) shows that regulation is not yet perfect, and has of course increased concern amongst the population.

1.2.3. Organic farming systems
These long-standing concerns about conventional agriculture led to the development of 'organic farming' (House of Lords, 1999). This is now a world-wide movement. It has certain characteristics that allow it to be clearly differentiated from conventional agriculture, though it is not easy to define precisely (Lampkin, 1990, p.2-6, and a forthcoming major review by Stockdale *et al*, 2000). In general its objectives are (1) to avoid the use of synthetic, highly toxic or soluble chemicals on crops and soils, (2) to ensure that the soil and its biota are healthy (the definition of 'soil health' is never very clear), (3) to use sound husbandry methods so that crops and stock are healthy, (4) to ensure the welfare of farm animals, (5) to use the biological natural cycles rather than distorting them. The International Federation of Agricultural Movements (IFOAM) has a rather general and lengthy definition, that states desirable outcomes rather than how to achieve them. The definition of the United States Department of Agriculture is terse and functional: "Organic farming is a production system which avoids or largely excludes the use of synthetically compounded fertilisers, pesticides, growth regulators and livestock feed additives. To the maximum extent feasible, organic farming systems rely on crop rotations, crop residues, animal manures, legumes, green manures, off-farm organic wastes, and aspects of biological pest control to maintain soil productivity and tilth, to supply plant nutrients and to control insects, weeds and other pests." However, there is no specific mention of animal welfare in this definition. European Union (1991) has also produced a lengthy but general definition.

Organic farmers usually have strong ethical and philosophical views, are very concerned about the environment , and lay stress on a holistic approach rather than the use of conventional 'reductionist' science. However, 'reductionist' scientists know perfectly well that complex systems are more than the sum of their parts, because of the interactions that occur, but their experience is that complex natural systems cannot be understood unless the component processes can be defined. Organic farmers also have a praiseworthy desire to care for the land rather than to exploit it, but many conventional farmers have similar views. The arguments for organic farming have been stated by the Soil Association (1999) and Lampkin (1990), with opposing arguments being given by MacKerron *et al* (1999).

In the UK the beginning of the movement was largely due to the Soil Association, that was formed in 1946. The UK rules must now in follow the EU rules, though they do not need to be identical to them. The operational control is with the UK Register of Organic Food Standards (UKROFS), an independent body set up at the request of MAFF. UKROFS standard methods must be followed by all farmers and growers who want to be approved as organic producers, and there is a well-established Certification Scheme under the Board of UKROFS. The Manual of UKROFS (1999) states: "the term organic foods ... means foods that have been produced in accordance with UKROFS Standards". UK organic foods are thus defined in terms of how they are produced, rather than by their properties.

On average organic produce sells for considerably higher producer prices than conventional (see Colman, this volume). This is because of the lower yield, which is rarely balanced by the savings on the inputs. This suggests that modern organic farming has its main place in affluent areas, where a difference in food prices is of little importance to consumers with large family incomes.

1.2.4. Integrated farming

This raises the question of whether there is a half-way house between using inputs to the full as in conventional agriculture, and not using many of them at all, as in organic agriculture. The approach in general is usually called "Integrated Farming Systems" or "Integrated Cropping Systems" (Marsh, 2000). Such agricultural systems aim to use inputs at minimum levels to produce a good yield, and only when they are necessary. All other proven procedures that are environment friendly, desirable for animal welfare or directed to ensure high food quality should also be used. There are several such integrated systems (MAFF, 1998). They are less well-defined than organic agriculture, and they depend more upon the judgement and attitudes of the individual farmer. Thus the "Linking Environment and Farming" (LEAF) system uses a Computerised Farm Audit to encourage and log compliance with the objectives of LEAF, but no member is at present obliged to follow precise rules. The definition adopted by the Integrated Arable Crop Production Alliance (the international association for integrated farming systems) members is: "A whole farm policy aiming to provide the basis for efficient and profitable production which is economically viable and environmentally responsible. It integrates beneficial natural processes into modern farming practices using advanced technology and aims to minimise the environmental risks while conserving, enhancing and recreating that which is of environmental importance".

An important principle for all farming systems is that the method of production and the origin of produce shall be clear to customers. There are now various Farm Assurance schemes that aim to do so, the largest having been set up by the NFU and a consortium of large food retailers (Early, 1998). These schemes aim to ensure quality and traceability, and thus acceptability to the customer. They therefore demand that all food must be produced by safe and environment-friendly methods, and that the provenance of a particular batch of food or food ingredients must be traceable from farm to shop. The exact protocols to be followed, and the degree of on-farm verification, still have to be finally determined in some cases, and these schemes are still at a formative stage. They can be seen as an approach to the Integrated systems, but with a special emphasis on customer relations and the retail outlets.

References

Carson, R. (1972) Silent spring. Houghton Mifflin, New York.

Cooke, G.W. (1967) The control of soil fertility. Crosby Lockwood, London

Early, R. (1998) Farm Assurance - benefit or burden? *Journal of the Royal Agricultural Society of England*, **159**, 32-43.

European Union (1992) *Regulation 2092/91 on organic production et. seq.* European Union, Brussels

Fussell G.E (1972) *The classical tradition in West European farming*. David & Charles, Newton Abbott

Hall, D. A. (1941) *Reconstruction and the land.* Macmillan, London.

House of Lords (1999) House of Lords Select Committee on European Communities Report (16th Report). *Organic Farming and the European Union*. Stationery Office, London.

Lampkin, N. (1990) *Organic farming.* 1994 Reprinting. Farming Press, Tonbridge, UK.

MacKerron D. K. L., Duncan J.M., Hillman J.R., Mackay G.R., Robinson D.J., Trudgill D.L and Wheatley R.J. (1999) Organic farming: science and belief. *Annual Report Scottish Crops Research Institute*, Dundee, 60-72.

Marsh J. (2000) *Integrated Farm Management - a farm strategy for the 21st Century*. LEAF, Royal Agricultural Society of England, Stoneleigh.

MAFF (1998) *Integrated Farming - agricultural research into practice*. Ministry of Agriculture, Fisheries and Food, London, pp 16.

Shoard M. (1980) *The theft of the countryside*. Temple Smith, London.

Tinker P.B. (1997) The environmental implications of intensified land use in developing countries. *Phil Trans Roy Soc. Lond B*, **352**, 1023-1033.

UKROFS (1999) *UK Register of Organic Food Standards (Manual)* MAFF Rm G43, Nobel House, 17, Smith Sq., London SW1 3JR

Chapter Two

Effects on Soils and Plant Nutrition

Professor D Greenland MA, DPhil, DAgSci, FIBiol, FWA, FRS

2.1. Plant nutrients

2.1.1. The essential role of plant nutrients

The overall picture of how plants derive their nutrients from the soil is well established (Marschner, 1995; Tinker and Nye, 2000). There are 13 chemical elements that are essential to all plants, with a few that are beneficial to certain species. The most common limitations to crop growth are due to shortages of nitrogen (N), phosphorus (P) and potassium (K). It is in relation to these three elements that most controversy has arisen, because almost all of the inorganic fertilisers applied in Britain have been used to remedy deficiencies of these elements. For each of them we will consider briefly their importance to the plant, their behaviour in the soil, and the sources from which they are derived. Later we will consider how these elements are provided by different farming systems, and the problems and advantages of conventional systems using inorganic fertilisers, organic systems, and integrated systems designed to combine the advantages and minimise the disadvantages associated with each of the other two.

2.1.2. Nitrogen

This is an essential component of proteins, enzymes, DNA and many other vital parts of plant metabolism. Its behaviour in the soil is complicated because most is present in organic compounds associated with the various forms of organic matter. But plants readily use only the inorganic forms, ammonium and nitrate. The amount of ammonium and nitrate in the soil normally accounts for only a small fraction of the total nitrogen present. Most is present as part of the soil organic matter. Before this nitrogen can be used by plants the organic matter must be decomposed by the soil animals and microorganisms. The nitrogen is initially released as ammonium, which is then converted by specific bacteria to nitrate. If there is more nitrate present than can be assimilated by the plants or the microorganisms which compete with the plants for the nitrogen supply the excess may be lost from the soil because all nitrates are readily washed into streams and rivers. Ammonium and nitrate may also be converted to gaseous forms and so lost to plants. The aim of nitrogen nutrition is to minimise losses, and ensure that there is always sufficient nitrate in the soil solution and within range of the roots to supply the immediate plant demand.

A few plant species, such as clovers, peas and beans, differ from other plants, because their nitrogen needs may be met by nitrogen "fixed" from the air by colonies of bacteria living in nodules on their roots. These plants (the legumes) may lose some of this fixed nitrogen into the soil solution, or it may be added to the organic nitrogen in the soil when the plant dies. Thus it can contribute not only to the plant supporting the nitrogen fixing bacteria but also to plants growing with it or after it.

2.1.3. Phosphorus

This is an essential component of DNA and pervasive within plant metabolic pathways. Its chemistry in the soil is also complicated. Its strong adsorption by the finer soil particles means that its rate of movement is very slow, and soils can be deficient even when containing substantial quantities of phosphorus, because the phosphate ions are unable to reach the plant roots at the necessary rate. In acid soils aluminium and iron may delay the uptake of phosphate by plants, and phosphate can also be precipitated as insoluble calcium phosphates in less acid soils.

Mineralised phosphorus does not necessarily reach plant roots because it can be adsorbed, precipitated, and assimilated by microorganisms. The plant can only obtain phosphorus from the soil solution, but mycorrhizal fungi associated with plant roots may help the plant by collecting phosphate from the soil solution and passing it on to the plant.

2.1.4. Potassium

This has a less complex chemical behaviour in the soil. Within the plant potassium remains in ionic form, and has important functions in control of ionic balance, acidity and osmotic pressure. Most of the potassium that is readily available to plants is adsorbed on the surfaces of the soil colloids, both organic and inorganic, and released to the soil solution by exchange with other cations. Much potassium may be present within the structures of minerals in the soil, but this potassium is strongly bound and only released by very slow chemical weathering of the minerals.

If the plants growing in the soil are to flourish it is essential that these major nutrients as well as the other ten are available in the soil solution. It is also essential that there are no toxic elements present, or others that may have a deleterious effect on the uptake of the nutrient elements. Most notable amongst these is aluminium, which is present in the soil solution when the soil is very acid.

Plant nutrition in soils is therefore by no means a simple subject and this must be borne in mind when considering the various agricultural systems. The aim must always be careful control of nutrients to optimise the supply to the crop to ensure its effective growth, and for this a scientific understanding is essential. In this brief introduction it is only possible to sketch the many processes which operate in soils and control the processes which determine the availability of nutrients to plants. There are many texts such as Wild (1988) which give a more complete account.

2.1.5. The sources of plant nutrients

The soil itself is of course the most important source of the elements required by crops. The amount of nutrients in the soil differ depending on the rocks from which the soil was formed, the vegetation and climate during soil formation, the deposition of material from the air or from water which may have flowed over the soil, and the length of time for which soil formation has occurred. If the soil has been used for agriculture it also depends on the crops which have been grown and the extent to which the nutrients absorbed from the soil by those crops have been returned or replaced i.e. on nutrient circulation between soil and vegetation.

Different farming systems are based on different methods of maintaining nutrients. The earliest systems mostly depended on abandoning the site that had been cultivated as soon as yields fell below an acceptable level and allowing the site to revert to natural vegetation. Nutrients were collected and absorbed by the regenerating vegetation and returned to the surface soil in the litter fall. After many years the soil returned to its precultivation state and could again be successfully cropped. Such systems of "shifting cultivation" can only be used where land is plentiful. Later methods based on stock farming used the animal to transfer nutrients from grazing land, that might be unsuitable for cultivation, to the cropped areas via the manure produced by the animals. Many present day organic farming systems are managed in various modifications of this essentially simple practice. In wetland areas, and the areas of the great river deltas, water may provide the necessary transfer agent, replenishing nutrients by carrying with it nutrients and sediments washed from soils in the upper reaches of the river systems.

Nitrogen is a special case because it may be fixed from the air, not only by symbiotic bacteria but also by some free-living bacteria. The free–living nitrogen fixers are seldom able to contribute more than about 10 kg/ha/year to the soil. The symbiotic bacteria may contribute up to 200 kg/ha/year provided that the legume with which they are associated is well supplied with other nutrients, particularly phosphorus, and grows well.

Only with the discovery of methods to mine or produce salts to use as cheap inorganic fertilisers did it become possible to replace the slow natural systems of restoring soil fertility with systems able to raise productivity substantially and immediately.

2.2. Soil improvement by organic manures, legume leys and green manures

2.2.1. The importance of soil organic matter (SOM)

If a soil is to remain productive over many years nutrients must be replaced and the soil must be maintained in a favourable physical condition. Cultivation of the soil is normally used to create a suitable structural condition for plant growth, but the condition can be unstable unless there is sufficient organic matter in the soil, or other stabilising agents such as free calcium carbonate or iron or aluminium oxides.

Organic materials are continuously added to most soils in the form of plant roots, animal wastes, litter and other debris, and are converted to the mixture of resistant organic compounds known as humus. The actual amount of total organic matter in the soil at any one time is the difference between the carbon added and the carbon lost as carbon dioxide due to the continuing activities of the soil population. All soils under a stable climate and constant vegetation, or for agricultural soils, a constant system of management, tend towards an equilibrium level of SOM when the rate of addition of carbon is equal to the rate of loss. The effects of organic matter on soil properties are described in

Table 2.1. Potential effects of soil organic matter on soil properties (Stevenson, 1982; Wild, 1988)

Chemical

Provides a balanced supply of some plant nutrients;
Retains nutrients against losses due to leaching;
Helps to mobilise nutrients from otherwise unavailable mineral sources;
Reduces phosphate sorption at mineral surfaces
Increases capacity of the soil to absorb pesticides and other pollutants, so preventing their entry to the wider environment;
Complexes aluminium, so reducing affects of acidity.

Physical

Stabilises the larger (transmission) pores, and so ensures water entry and good drainage and the free movement of air and water, and eases the growth of plant roots;
Strengthens soil aggregates against dispersion by raindrop impact, and so reduces run-off and erosion;
Increases retention of water available to plants.

Biological

Feeds the soil animals and micro-organisms and so ensures the release of the nutrients contained in the organic matter in forms usable by plants;
The soil fauna create the transmission pores;
An active population competes with any introduced pathogens and so reduces the chances of plant and animal infection;
Supports the soil population and may increase its diversity.

most soil science texts and are summarised in Table 2.1. There is now also strong interest in the sequestration of carbon from carbon dioxide, and a build-up of SOM in soil is one way of doing this.

In soils that are naturally favourable to plant growth the physical and biological effects of the organic matter may be unimportant if sufficient nutrients are available. However where physical and biological effects limit crop yields, organic matter is important. It is also essential where the soil contains too few nutrients in inorganic forms.

2.2.2. The dynamics of soil organic matter

All fertile soils are normally a teeming mass of biological activity. Many factors affect the soil population, and hence the rate at which added organic matter decomposes, and the proportion of carbon added in manures which remains in the soil and contributes to the physical and biological behaviour of the soil. For instance, when a soil is cultivated, the rate of decomposition increases because more SOM is exposed to breakdown by the soil population. Conversely, if a soil is left undisturbed under natural vegetation or pasture, organic matter accumulates because the rate of addition is higher than when arable crops are grown, and because the rate of decomposition and loss is lower.

The greater the amount of nitrogen available to the soil population, the more biomass and humus are formed, because nitrogen is an essential component. Thus when nitrogen fixation occurs, more SOM accumulates. When the soil is cultivated this nitrogen is released to the succeeding crop as the SOM level falls.

The changes in SOM have been measured in the continuous wheat and barley experiments started at the Rothamsted Experiment Station 150 years ago. The annual addition of 35t/ha of farmyard manures has trebled the amount of SOM in the soil, but fertilisers have increased the SOM only very slightly, compared to cropping without additions of manure or fertilisers because the quantity of organic matter added to the soil as crop residues was much less than the 35 t/ha added as farmyard manure. The untreated plots have remained at the same low level of organic matter as when the experiment started, because the land had already been used for arable crops for 200 years. Wheat yields on the manured plots have increased from less than 2 t/ha to over 6 t/ha, and on the fertilised plots to over 8 t/ha, but on the untreated plots they have remained close to the original 2 t/ha. In the barley experiment, the manure additions were discontinued on some plots in 1872, and the soil organic matter levels and yields then fell, as would be expected (Jenkinson, 1991). Using data from such long-term experiments quantitative models of the organic carbon and nitrogen changes under different farming systems can be constructed (Young, 1994; Chambers *et al*, 1999).

2.2.3. Legumes and ley farming

The use of animal manures is not the only organic option. Ley farming systems in which arable cropping is alternated with legume based pastures can also build soil organic matter (see Maxwell and Goddard, this volume). These systems are now recognised as the practicable basis for most organic farming systems in the UK. The pasture legumes may add 100 to 200 kg/ha of nitrogen per season to the soil, as a component of soil organic matter. There have been many studies of such systems in which yields from an arable crop grown after a grass-legume pasture have been compared with continuous arable cropping using nitrogen fertilisers. Most of the studies have confirmed that a higher organic matter status is achieved by ley farming. Nevertheless, except on a few soils of poor physical condition, such as some heavy silty clays, rather little yield advantage has been found for the ley-arable systems compared with well fertilised and continuously cropped arable, even though the physical condition of the soil improved (Eagle, 1975). Overall the economic productivity of most ley-arable systems was significantly lower, because on few arable soils in the UK are physical or biological conditions a limiting factor for crop production.

However in some ley-arable experiments started at Rothamsted in 1949 it was found that when wheat yields exceeded 7 t/ha, small yield advantages were obtained for the arable crops in the rotations which included the ley (Johnston *et al*, 1994). It was concluded that at these higher yield levels the physical or possibly the biological conditions under continuous arable cropping became limiting. The system was not wholly organic as P and K fertilisers were applied to both the leys and the arable phase.

Legume crops such as peas and beans can contribute 50 to 60 kg/ha of N to a cereal crop, and add a similar amount to the soil, while meeting their own requirements for nitrogen (Peoples and Craswell, 1992). Pasture legumes such as red clover may also be grown as green manures for one or two years, and ploughed into the soil, when they may contribute as much as 200 kg of nitrogen to a following cereal crop (Cormack, 1999). But the needs of the legumes as well as the succeeding crops for other nutrient elements must come from the soil or other sources, normally current applications of manure or fertiliser or residues from fertilisers.

Legumes will only fix nitrogen from the air actively if there is a sufficiently high level of phosphorus available in the soil. Fortunately the long use of superphosphate in the UK has increased the levels of available phosphate sufficiently to ensure that many pasture soils will support the growth of clovers and their symbiont nitrogen fixers for a long time without further phosphate addition. Potassium and sulphur have also been built to levels that will sustain productive pastures for some years to come. The value of these residues will in time be exhausted, and ultimately more nutrients will be needed. The major long-term difficulty with pasture based systems is that, of the major plant nutrients, only nitrogen can be taken from the air. Of course, if phosphatic and potassium fertilisers are acceptable for use there is no fundamental problem in the greater use of such ley-arable farming systems. Nevertheless in assessing the economics of organic ley-arable systems the declining yields which will occur as the residual effects of the earlier fertiliser applications disappear must be taken into account.

2.3. Farming with fertilisers

2.3.1. Early fertiliser work

Sir John Lawes, who founded the research at Rothamsted, showed in 1840 that bones treated with sulphuric acid greatly stimulated crop growth. The "superphosphate" produced required far less labour to spread on the land than farm-yard manure (Dyke, 1993). The improvement was greater if manures high in nitrogen such as "hoof and horn"or guano were used as well as the superphosphate produced. Some nitrogen salts, such as saltpetre or sodium and potassium nitrates from Chile and elsewhere, occur naturally. These were used experimentally and their effectiveness in providing nitrogen to plants established, but it was not until relatively cheap methods for fixing nitrogen from the air were discovered in the 20th century that various inorganic salts of nitrogen became generally and cheaply available. During the 1939-1945 war when as much food as possible had to be grown in Britain use of inorganic nitrogen started to rise dramatically (Figure 2.1 overleaf).

The rise continued after the war stimulated by government subsidy, introduced in wartime. The average annual application of NPK as fertilisers for winter wheat grew from 51 kg/ha in 1944 to 225 kg/ha in 1994, but has since fallen gradually as greater efforts have been made to reduce environmental effects and increase efficiency.

The residual value of nutrients applied other than nitrogen has been shown to be high (Johnston, 1970; Wild, 1988), so that the productivity of almost all farmed land in the UK has increased greatly during the 20th century, making farming profitable and ensuring cheap food for all. The reserves of available nutrients in the soil have increased substantially, so that current reductions in fertiliser use in organic farming have had much less impact than they would otherwise have done.

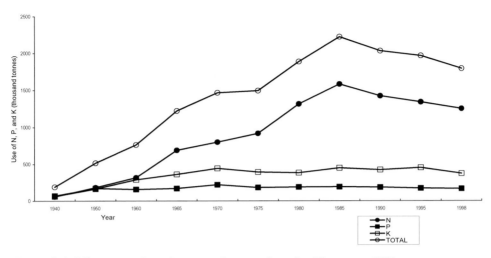

Figure 2.1. Nitrogen, phosphorus and potassium fertiliser use, UK

2.3.2. Comparisons of the effects of fertilisers and manures on yields

In the experiments at Rothamsted mentioned above, the effects of 35 t/ha/year of farmyard manure on cereal yields have been compared with yields from plots receiving large additions of inorganic fertilisers. In 1968, the yields with the inorganics exceeded those with the manure by around 1 t/ha, and analyses of the crops indicated that the nitrogen supply from the manure was inadequate. A supplement of 96.4kg/ha of inorganic nitrogen was then applied with the manure. This increased the yields from the manured plots so that subsequently they have slightly exceeded those from the inorganics only plots (Johnston, quoted by Greenland, 1997).

The heavily fertilised plots receiving no organic additions show no indication of declining yields or crop quality. There were however some difficulties, on both the manured and fertilised plots, in controlling weeds when herbicides were not used.

One must ask if the results from the Rothamsted experiments are applicable to other crops, soils and weather conditions, or with different levels and types of fertilisers. The farming community became seriously concerned in the 1960's that on some soils significant damage was caused by modern intensive farming methods when insufficient organic matter was returned to the soil. The report of the Strutt Committee (MAFF, 1970) showed the extent of concern, but concluded there was no hard scientific evidence of widespread serious soil damage. Experiments at Rothamsted with barley gave very similar results to those obtained with wheat, but with potatoes, a crop more sensitive to structural conditions in the soil (Powlson and Johnston, 1994), yields were greater from the plots receiving the manure. Long-term experiments at many other sites have mostly shown that the beneficial effects of inorganic fertilisers on crop yields are the norm, and that the advantages continue for many years. The most notable exception is at Woburn, 20 miles from Rothamsted, where the climate is similar but the soils sandier, more acid and yields generally lower.

Until lime was applied yields fell on the fertilised plots and on the manured plots, but the rate of decline was slower where manures were used.

Several other examples of the inability of inorganic fertilisers alone to maintain soil productivity have been found in relatively poor acid soils in other parts of the world (Greenland, 1997). Unfortunately far too few experiments have been conducted to determine where organic manuring is essential to maintain yields, or what is the critical level of SOM below which yields from those soils cannot be maintained. More data are also needed to establish what levels of SOM are needed to avoid undesirable environmental effects or unacceptable changes in the diversity and size of the soil populations.

2.3.3. Dangers of excessive use of fertilisers

Modern farming methods have been extensively criticised for polluting the soil and the environment, primarily because it is believed that nitrate derived from fertilisers enters the water supply. Nitrate in the soil arises not only from nitrogen fertilisers but also from organic material already present in the soil, and from organic manures added to the soil, as discussed earlier. Correct timing of the application of fertilisers or manures, so that most nitrate is present at the time of maximum plant uptake, minimises leaching of nitrate. Leaching losses can be further reduced if "Precision Agriculture" methods are used, in which the rates of fertiliser applied are not only related to individual fields but also tailored to soil conditions and likely crop offtake at the site of application. Such precise methods cannot be used with organic manures because of their different water and nutrient contents, as well as the problems of the large bulk that has to be spread. Further, their application is most conveniently done in the autumn and winter when animals are housed, and this can lead to large losses when rapid mineralisation occurs in the spring. It is obviously in the interests of the farmer, as well as the environment, to avoid these losses and ensure that as much of the nitrogen as possible is absorbed by the crop.

Rates of crop recovery of nitrogen may be measured by labelling the applied nitrogen with the stable isotope of nitrogen. This has shown that recovery rates differ considerably depending not only on the soil characteristics, but also on the source of the nitrogen, the timing of the application and the method of distribution. Commonly about 40% to 60% is recovered in the crop, part is assimilated into the soil organic matter, part lost by leaching, and a small part lost by conversion to gaseous forms. The proportions depend on soil and weather conditions. A number of rigorously conducted experiments (Addiscott *et al*, 1991) have shown that the nitrate derived from fertiliser that entered waterways, although dependent on soil and seasonal conditions, was often less than 6% of the amount applied.

Losses by drainage from permanent pastures and leys are much less than when other crops are grown, but cultivating soils after pasture or a ley always leads to large losses, as the flush of nitrate mineralised from the accumulated soil organic matter is released. Most nitrate in groundwaters in chalk and other aquifers accumulated when old grasslands were ploughed during the war, and has subsequently contributed to the nitrate levels in water supplies. Nevertheless there has been a tendency in the media and elsewhere to place the major responsibility for nitrate pollution on increased use of nitrogen fertilisers. Fertilisers certainly contribute, but much has also arisen from the cultivation of leys and pastures, as well as from organic manures, and the mineralisation of nitrogen in organic matter accumulated in the soil prior to its use for arable cultivation (Addiscott *et al*, 1991).

Gaseous losses of nitrogen can make a significant contribution to global warming because the very effective greenhouse gas, nitrous oxide, is evolved when soil microbes cause denitrification (Smith and Adah, 1990). Methane, another effective greenhouse gas, may also be evolved. Both nitrous oxide and methane losses are likely to be greater from organic farming than conventional farming, because the bacteria that produce them require easily decomposed organic material to support their activity. Burford (1976) and Scott *et al* (2000) have shown that nitrous oxide evolution from heavy applications of organic manures resulted in greater evolution of nitrous oxide than when equivalent amounts of inorganic nitrogen were applied. Volatilisation of ammonia, that also has undesirable environmental effects, is again much greater from manures.

In contrast to nitrate, phosphate is strongly adsorbed by the soil. Thus when phosphate fertilisers are added to the soil, most is adsorbed or precipitated as inorganic salts. Some may also be assimilated by soil organisms. Thus although large quantities of phosphate fertilisers are added to the soil, most of the phosphate remains in the soil. The precipitated and adsorbed phosphate will however maintain a low concentration in the soil solution for many years. It is this residual phosphate which is mainly sustaining crop production as use of phosphate fertilisers is reduced or eliminated in organic farming systems.

Eutrophication due to phosphate has mostly arisen when effluents from intensive animal production systems have passed directly into streams and rivers, when phosphate fertilisers have been spread on the soil surface without incorporation in the soil, and when phosphate fertilisers are used on very sandy soils that contain few colloids to immobilise the phosphate. Research conducted in the past ten years has established that phosphate leached out of the soil may be sufficient to contribute to eutrophication of some surface waters (Tunney *et al*, 1997, p.459). Nevertheless the total quantities of phosphate reaching waterways after the water has filtered through the soil are a very small fraction of the total applied, whether applied as fertiliser or manure.

Potassium fertilisers are also used in large amounts. They are not known to pose either an environmental or health risk. The proportion of potassium in animal manures tends to be high in relation to the nitrogen content, so that potassium in excess of the plant requirement may be present for cereal crops, although not for root crops which have a greater potassium demand.

2.4. Farming without manufactured fertilisers

2.4.1. Using animal manures

For any farming system to produce crops sustainably, plant nutrients have to be added to the soil to replace those lost from the system. In conventional systems this is by the use of fertilisers. In organic systems it is by the use of organic manures and some naturally occurring minerals, such as rock phosphates and sylvinite, a mixture of potassium and sodium chlorides. Use of rock phosphate and sylvinite, guano, fish meal and blood and bone, permissible in organic farming systems according to UKROFS, will help to maintain productivity. The slower release of the phosphate from the rock phosphate, means that the concentration maintained in the soil solution remains less than optimum, and hence yields are lower than those attainable when inorganic fertilisers are used.

Sylvinite is easily soluble, and contains more chloride per unit weight of potassium than does purified potassium chloride in conventional fertiliser. Soft rock phosphate can be a useful supplier of phosphorus in acid soils but "no PR (phosphate rock) source is effective in soils having pH levels above 5.5 to 6.0" (Engelstad and Terman, 1980). Most UK arable soils are close to or above this pH level. The difference between these rock phosphates and conventional superphosphate is essentially that some of the calcium has been removed, to render the phosphate more soluble in neutral or alkaline soils. It is difficult to see any scientific reason why the simple operations carried out to convert these raw natural sources into the fertilisers of commerce should be looked upon with such suspicion. Their effects on nutritional value of the produce are discussed later in this volume.

Both sylvinite and rock phosphate are of course "non-sustainable resources", being found in limited deposits. In fact the total amounts of phosphate rock that can be used to make conventional fertiliser are much greater than the soft rock phosphate that can be used for organic farming.

The amount of organic manure of 35 t/ha/year used in the Rothamsted experiments is close to the upper limit of what it is normally practicable to incorporate, and is usually insufficient to supply enough nitrogen to raise yields to the present UK average of 8 t/ha. This rate of manure addition is also unlikely to be sufficient to replace the losses of phosphorus in crop removals. On most farms where sufficient animals are kept so that manure applications of 35 t/ha are possible, it will probably be 100 years or more before the soil organic matter approaches an equilibrium content such that yields of 6 t/ha of wheat or its equivalent can be achieved without application of additional nitrogen, or inclusion of a legume in the system. To attain more than 6 t/ha of grain in continuous organic farming systems would require that the animal manures were supplemented by nitrogen from other sources. UKROFS requires that only manure coming from extensive husbandry practices is used, which reduces the amount of manure available to a small fraction of the total.

The lack of evidence of any unfavourable effects on crop production due to the long-continued use of inorganic fertilisers has led some to conclude that not only have the inorganic fertilisers improved yields, but also that the organic additions have had no beneficial effects other than those arising from the nutrients contained. In the 1950's this certainly led to some vigorous arguments that the proponents of organic farming were wrong in asserting that organic matter additions other than those from crop residues were essential to sustainable production. The fact that the manured plots had to be given inorganic nitrogen if yields were to match those obtained from the fertilised plots supported this argument.

Table 2.2. Ranges of heavy metal concentrations in sewage sludges, fertilisers and farmyard manures (Alloway, 1990) and permitted concentrations in soils amended with sewage sludge (Houghton, 1996)

All data as mg/kg. (Note that topsoil on 1 ha. of arable land weighs about 2,000,000 kg.)

Element	Sewage sludge	Phosphate fertiliser	Nitrate fertiliser	Farmyard manure	Permitted soil conc.
Cadmium	1-3410	0.1-170	0.5-8.5	0.1-0.8	3
Cobalt	1-260	5.4-12	5.4-12	0.3-2.4	-
Chromium	8-40600	66-245	3.2-1.9	1.1-55	400
Copper	50-8000	1-300	-	2-172	135
Mercury	0.1-55	0.01-1.2	0.3-2.9	0.01-3.6	-
Manganese	60-3900	40-2000	-	30-969	-
Nickel	6-5300	7-38	7-34	2.1-30	75
Lead	29-3600	7-225	2-27	1.1-2.7	300
Zinc	91-49000	50-1450	1-42	15-566	300

2.4.2. Using other manures

There has for long been public interest in the possibility of using wastes to recycle the essential nutrients for crop production, not least because it offers one route to establish a "closed nutrient cycling system". Use of composted household waste is restricted according to its origin and content of some heavy metals. Not mentioned by UKROFS, but listed amongst prohibited materials by the Soil Association and the EU are sewage sludge, effluents and sludge based composts, although the nutrient contents of these materials would be an important source of nutrient additions. Unfortunately, although containing a high concentration of plant nutrients, sewage sludge normally contains a high concentration of heavy metals, especially zinc, due to disposal of domestic and industrial wastes into sewage systems (Table 2.2). Although the sludge can be "cleaned" of heavy metals, this adds a significant cost. There are of course also human and animal health hazards associated with the use of manures and sludge due to the possible presence of pathogens (Kofoed *et al*, 1986; see Williams *et al*, this volume).

Most governments and the European Commission have set standards for the maximum levels of heavy metals that can be established in soils when sewage sludge is used as a soil amendment (Alloway, 1990; Houghton, 1996). These standards are currently under review.

Concentrations of heavy metals in fertilisers are mostly lower than in sewage sludges (Table 2.2), although some sources of phosphates used in the preparation of fertilisers contain relatively high levels of cadmium. However the quantities of sludge and manure applied per hectare are very much greater than the amounts of fertiliser applied, so that the spread of heavy metals by sewage and manure compared with inorganic fertilisers is even greater than the relative concentrations suggest.

2.4.3. The fate of pesticides

The fate of pesticides in the soil is quite complex (Graham-Bryce, 1981; Pain *et al*, 1991). Most concern about modern farming methods has arisen from the use of pesticides. Their effects on pathogens and biodiversity are considered elsewhere (see Plumb, this volume), but it is appropriate to consider briefly here their fate when added to the soil, either deliberately as with herbicides or inadvertently when crops are sprayed. They may be decomposed by soil organisms, adsorbed by the organic or inorganic constituents of the soil, leached out of the soil, or volatilised. They may be toxic to some components of the soil population and thereby cause a change in the balance and size of the population. Each of these processes can be important in determining the fate of any individual pesticide, and it is important not to generalise too readily about any specific pesticide because of their very different chemical constitution, physical properties and biological effects (Goring and Hamaker, 1972). However, it is safe to say that under current regulations, there is at present little hard evidence of damage to productivity or the soil environment, unless they are grossly misused (see Greenwood, this volume).

2.5. Farming with minimum levels of fertilisers

Although inorganic fertilisers are very effective in increasing crop yields, and generally do so very economically, the spreading of large quantities of chemicals on the land has been regarded by the proponents of organic farming as highly undesirable. Nevertheless yields in the UK are now higher than they have ever been, largely because fertilisers solve the problems of nutrient depletion more efficiently and effectively than other methods. However most gardeners as well as farmers know that organic manures make the soil more friable and easier to cultivate, and that an active soil population keeps the soil open and porous. They also recognise that these conditions are related to the maintenance of adequate levels of humus in the soil, and that this in turn requires the regular addition of substantial quantities of organic matter, as compost, green manure or other manures. Organic farming systems normally help to maintain or increase the level of soil organic matter, particularly if legumes are included in the farming system. But yields will not be sustained unless provision is made to ensure that the levels of plant available phosphate and potassium do not decline. Some plants may be especially active in releasing adsorbed phosphate from soil colloids, and organic manures may also promote such releases, but this is a form of soil mining that cannot be sustained indefinitely. Augmenting soil phosphorus levels with rock phosphate and soil potassium levels with naturally occurring potassium minerals such as sylvinite, as permitted by UKROFS and the EU organic farming regulations, will increase or at least reduce the rate of loss of these elements. However, the use of these materials in the UK at present is quite small.

There is good economic sense in reducing the amounts of chemicals applied to levels where they produce optimal economic advantage, without causing significant environmental problems. Such an approach is used in "integrated crop management" (ICM) or Integrated Farming Systems (IFS) (see Tinker, this volume). The main problem is deciding the smallest amount of fertiliser required on a particular field in a particular year to give and sustain the optimum economic yield. This depends on the past history of fertilising and cropping, as well as the soil type, the crop to be grown, the weather expected in the growing period, as well as economic factors. Thus the prediction of what is the optimum amount of fertiliser to use is far from simple. Advice is available, from ADAS and others, and may be supported by recently developed computer models. However many farmers still tend to take a cautious approach based on past experience, and apply more than the predicted requirement. If organic manures are applied as well as fertilisers, their nutrient contents must be allowed for when calculating optimum fertiliser rates. The organic manures will also reduce the risk of crop failure, and build the nutrient as well as organic matter content of the soil. Thus the best method of maintaining the long-term productivity of soils is by a combination of organic additions and use of mineral fertilisers, as in ICM/IFS methods.

2.6. Conclusion

There are advantages and disadvantages to the use of both conventional and organic farming systems. This chapter has focused on arable production systems and horticultural systems have not been considered, as they cover a relatively small proportion of soils used for crop production in Britain. Horticultural crops have more specific and greater nutrient requirements than most arable crops, and are more sensitive to soil physical conditions. Thus it is probable that for horticultural crops the balance of advantage is with integrated systems. For arable production the great advantage of conventional systems using fertilisers and pesticides is that the methods are simple and economic to use, the crop is well fed and vigorous, and the effects of weed competition, insect attack and disease problems, minimised. Continued use of these methods in arable agriculture does reduce the soil organic matter content, and this may cause a deterioration in some soil properties. However under UK conditions the changes usually have little if any effect on present or future productivity of the soil, and the deleterious effects are mostly reversible (Greenland, 1980). Far from causing declines in crop yields as some had predicted, modern farming methods have had a continuing and positive effect on yields, and, because malnutrition has been largely eliminated, on plant and human health. The balance of advantage in arable farming probably lies with integrated and conventional systems.

Organic farming systems have distinct disadvantages due to the costs of collection and distribution of the manures, and if these systems are to be more widely used, to insufficient availability of the required quantities. The amounts which must be applied to ensure an adequate nutrient supply are very high, and were it not for the build-up of nutrients in most arable soils in Britain due to fertiliser use, nutrient levels would be quite inadequate for economic crop production. The possibly large contents of heavy metals in sewage, and the potential problems of the spread of disease organisms, limit its wider use. The problems of nitrate contamination of groundwaters have been shown to be due as much to mineralisation of organic nitrogen in the soil as to nitrates derived directly from fertiliser nitrogen. Most of the present evidence indicates that the emission of greenhouse gases is greater when organic farming methods are practised than when conventional farming systems are used, although in the long-term the sequestration of carbon in the subsoil will be greater under organic farming systems. The physical condition of the soil improves when organic matter levels are relatively high. This reduces the energy needed for cultivation, but seldom has a positive effect on yields under English conditions. Use of legumes as cover crops or in ley farming systems have distinct advantages in minimising the need for inorganic nitrogen. But while they can add nitrogen by biological nitrogen fixation, they are dependent on adequate levels of phosphorus and other nutrients. The logical conclusion is that soil fertility and crop production should be supported by the integrated use of organic manures and inorganic fertilisers, based on well established scientific principles.

In this chapter it has not been possible to discuss many aspects of the different cropping systems, notably the importance of crop rotations, the details of soil processes and how they are affected by soil organisms and soil organic matter. Much has still to be learnt. Such knowledge can only be obtained by the continued and rigorous management and careful scientific study such as has been accorded the Rothamsted experiments.

References

Addiscott, T. M., Whitmore, A. P.and Powlson, D. S. (1991) *Farming, Fertilizers and the Nitrate Problem.* CAB International, Wallingford.

Alloway, B.J. (1990) *Heavy Metals in Soils. Blackies*, London and Wileys, New Jersey.

Burford, J.R. (1976) Effect of a heavy application of cow slurry to grassland on the composition of the soil atmosphere. *J.Sci. Food Agric.* **27**, 115-126.

Chambers, B.J., Lord, E.I., Nicholson, F.A. and Smith, K.A. (1999) Predicting nitrogen availability and losses following application of organic manures to arable land. *Soil Use and Management*, **15**, 137-143.

Cormack, W. (1997) The ADAS Terrington stockless organic arable project. Proceedings of Organic Farming - Science into Practice 1997. Royal Agricultural Society of England, Stoneleigh.

Dyke, G.V. (1993) *John Lawes of Rothamsted: Pioneer of science, farming and industry.* Hoos Press, Harpenden.

Eagle, D.J. (1975) ADAS ley fertility experiments. In: *Soil Physical Conditions and Crop Production. MAFF Technical Bulletin Number 29.* HMSO, London.

Engelstad, O.P. and Terman, G.L. (1980) Agronomic effectiveness of phosphate fertilisers. In: *The role of phosphorus in agriculture* (Eds. F.E. Khasawneh, E.C. Sample and E.J. Kamprath). American Society of Agronomy, Madison USA., pp 311-332.

Graham-Bryce, I.G. (1981) The Behaviour of pesticides in soil. In: *The Chemistry of Soil Processes* (Ed. D.J. Greenland and M.H.B. Hayes). Wileys, Chichester, pp 621-670.

Goring, C.A.I. and Hamaker, J.W. (1972) *Organic Chemicals in the Soil Environment.* Dekker, New York.

Greenland, D.J. (1980) Soil damage by intensive arable cultivation:temporary or permanent? *Phil. Trans. Roy. Soc., London, B,* **281**, 193-208.

Greenland, D.J. (1997) Soil conditions and plant growth. *Soil Use and Management*, **13**, 169-177.

Houghton, J. (1996) Royal Commission on Environmental Pollution. 19th Report. *Sustainable Use of Soil.* HMSO, London.

Jenkinson, D.S. (1991) The Rothamsted long-term experiments: are they still of use? *Agronomy Journal*, **83**, 2-10.

Johnston, A.E. (1970) The value of residues from long-period manuring at Rothamsted and Woburn. *Rothamsted Experimental Station Report for 1969*, Part 2, 5-90.

Johnston, A.E., McEwen, J., Lane, P.W., Hewitt, M.V., Poulton, P.R. and Yeoman, D.P. (1994) Effects of one to six year old ryegrass-clover leys on soil nitrogen and on the subsequent yields and fertiliser nitrogen requirements of the arable sequence winter wheat, potatoes, winter wheat, winter beans (Vicia faba) grown on a sandy loam soil. *Journal of Agricultural Science*, **122**, 73-89

Marschner, H. (1995) *Mineral Nutrition of Higher Plants*. Academic Press, London.

MAFF (1970) *Modern farming and the soil*. Agricultural Advisory Council. HMSO, London.

Kofoed, A. Dam, Williams, J.H. and L'Hermite, P. (1986) *Efficient Land Use of Sludge and Manure*. Elsevier, London and New York.

Pain, B., Jarvis, S.C. and Clements, R. (1991) Impact of agricultural practices on soil pollution. *Outlook on Agriculture*, **20**, 153-160.

Peoples, M. B. and Craswell, E. (1992) Biological nitrogen fixation; investments, expectations and actual contributions to agriculture. *Plant and Soil*, **141**, 13-39.

Powlson, D.S. and Johnston, A.E. (1994) Long-term field experiments: Their importance in understanding sustainable soil use. In: *Soil Resilience and Sustainable Land Use* (Eds. D.J. Greenland and I. Szabolcs). CAB International, Wallingford pp 367-394.

Scott, A., Ball, B. C., Crighton, L.J. and Aitken, M. N. (2000) Nitrous oxide and carbon dioxide emissions from grassland amended with sewage sludge. *Soil Use and Management*, **16**, 36-41.

Smith, K.A. and Adah, J.R.M. (1990) Losses of nitrogen by denitrification and emissions of nitrogen oxides by soils. *Fertiliser Society, Proceedings, no. 299*.

Stevenson, F.J. (1982) *Humus Chemistry; Genesis, Composition, Reactions*. Wiley, New York.

Tinker, P.B. and Nye, P.H. (2000) *Solute Movement in the Rhizosphere*. Oxford University Press, New York.

Tunney, H., Carton, O.T., Brookes, P.C. and Johnston, A.E. (eds) (1997) *Phosphorus Loss from Soil to Water*. CAB International, Wallingford.

Wild, A. (1988) *Russell's Soil Conditions and Plant Growth*, 11th edition. Longmans, Harlow, and Wileys, New York.

Young, A. (1994) Modelling changes in soil properties. In: *Soil Resilience and Sustainable Land Use* (Eds. D.J. Greenland and I. Szabolcs) CAB International, Wallingford, pp 423-447.

Chapter Three

Pests and Diseases

Professor R Plumb BSc, PhD, CBiol, FIBiol, FRGS

3.1. Introduction

The growth of genetically similar plants over large areas, as in most of current UK agriculture, is intended to provide conditions that favour some species (the crops) over others. Some of these other species are identified as pests[1], because they decrease the productivity, usefulness and value of those crops to man. This pattern of cropping has been associated with a simplification of the rotations used, especially a decrease in grass/clover leys and a move from mixed to all-arable farming, the maintenance of which is dependent upon external inputs to minimise loss due to the 'pests' that develop within the system.

The use of these inputs has to be judged against the benefits of their use, allowing for some use as insurance. There has also been a geographical shift in farming enterprises resulting from the ability to overcome pest constraints, coupled with price structures. Thus, 20-30 years ago arable crops were comparatively rare in the west of the UK, except when grown for feeding on farm, at least in part because conditions in the west favour pests and made much commercial arable crop production uneconomic. However, as prices have declined the cost:benefit analysis has changed throughout agriculture, and farming is seeking ways to remain profitable in the new market environment. This, at least partly, accounts for the move into organic production. However, there are many organic growers who see organic farming as more than just a system for producing food (see Tinker, this volume). This contributes to the difficulties in making comparisons between the relatively rigid organic approach to crop production and protection, and that adopted by most growers of exploiting the flexibility that modern inputs offer.

3.2. Crop protection strategies

Farmers seek simple solutions to complex problems. Crop protection problems are complex, are often understood only at the level of yield loss, and differ between farms. Pesticides were, in some quarters, hailed as the 'magic bullet' that would solve crop protection problems, but over the years their disadvantages as well as their merits have become clearer.

Crop protection has always required a combined approach. In contrast to what appears in the media, methods of crop production and protection,

---

[1] *Throughout the text pests refers to all causes of yield loss due to vertebrates, invertebrates, fungi, bacteria, viruses and weeds, and pesticides to those materials used to restrict their development or kill them or prevent their spread.*

including intensive, conventional production and organic farming, have much in common, although those at the extremes might not recognise each other as being in the same business. The main differences are in the relative emphasis given to the different options available to achieve the same end, making a living out of food production. If conserving or preserving a particular type of landscape or environment also has priority, then a different balance must be found.

All growers seek to use the great advances that have been made in plant breeding over the last 50-100 years, especially improvements in resistance to invertebrate pests and fungal diseases, and increases in potential productivity. These newly incorporated resistances, often from wild relatives, have also encouraged the development of pests that can overcome those resistances. So novel sources and combinations of resistance and ways of using them have been sought. When this has not been possible, or where yield is still being lost at an uneconomic level, the main alternative approach has been the use of pesticides.

Pesticides are not a 20th century invention and are not exclusively used in agriculture. The earliest pesticides, derived from "natural materials" such as sulphur, copper and arsenic, were extremely toxic to a wide range of pests but their discovery and use owed little to knowledge of the biology of the pest. Some are still, if only for a short while, acceptable as a last resort in organic production, but they scarcely match the environmentally friendly image so widely portrayed and perceived as characterising this form of agriculture. The modern era of pesticides dates from the last 50-60 years and some of the early materials, notably DDT, were extremely effective. However, as their prolonged use showed, they had undesirable effects higher up the food chain (Metcalf, 1986). More modern pesticides are also very effective, often very specific, and are usually less persistent than earlier materials. They also have to undergo extensive and detailed toxicological and efficacy testing before they can be used (see Williams *et al,* this volume).

To be successful crop protection decisions need to be underpinned by a sound knowledge of the direct interactions between the crop and their pests. The organic grower tries to manipulate the environment of the crop to minimise pest, disease and weed effects so that no intervention is necessary, or only as a last resort, and only using those materials permitted by UKROFS and monitored through the various certification schemes (Anon, 1999; Lampkin and Measures, 1999). The conventional grower tries to minimise the need to control pests, but also seeks to know whether and when chemical intervention is necessary. Between the conventional and organic approaches there is a whole range of methods often found under the titles of Integrated Crop Management, Integrated Pest Management, Integrated Farming Systems, and Lower Input (Sustainable) Farming (see Tinker, this volume). The position of any one enterprise along this continuum depends on personal approaches (philosophy), location and past history, but principally on economics. Farmers can only do what they do if it makes a profit over the short to medium term. Sustainability in this sense is a stark choice of survival or not.

There is little reason why research, at the basic level of interactions between components of the farming environment should not be useful and relevant to all agriculture. However, in comparisons of specific approaches to individual crop protection problems, the usual reductionist scientific methods may not be very useful. The argument often put by the organic grower is that such comparisons are invalid, as they do not accept the premises on which the comparisons are based. There is much truth in this. It is very difficult to draw any conclusions about the relative effectiveness of a system that claims to have ensured, largely through cultural methods, that pests were below threshold levels, with a system in which pesticides have achieved the same result (Leake, 1996). This is especially so when the comparisons do not address the added 'external' value claimed in environmental benefits for organic production methods.

That pests are important and need to be suppressed is not in dispute. Conventional approaches to farming do not prevent losses caused by pests but the proportion of these losses attributable to different pest components differs among crops, regions and seasons. It also seems clear that the proportion of crop lost in organic systems is, on average, smaller than in conventional systems. This is largely because the yield potential of organic crops is generally smaller, but also because organically grown crops are generally less susceptible to pests, especially diseases, than those grown conventionally. Much of this difference is due to the nitrogen status of the crop. Crops well supplied with fertiliser nitrogen provide a much better host for fungi than crops grown organically, but evidence for the effects of other major nutrients is much less clear (Jenkyn and Bainbridge, 1978).

As conventional agriculture in the UK is highly dependent on pesticides and cereals occupy by far the largest area of cropped land, they are therefore the largest recipients of pesticide treatments (Table 3.1.). However, it is interesting that the real cost of pesticides used in the UK has barely increased in the last 20 years, as the current value of the £460 million spent in 1999 is almost the same at constant values as the £180 million spent in 1980. Agriculture is not the only user of pesticides. Local authorities and Railtrack are large users of herbicides, which are usually applied to free-draining surfaces such as pavements, gutters and track beds.

Herbicides and fungicides dominate the area sprayed whereas insecticides are only a minor component, but are important in many seed treatments. However, in terms of quantity of active ingredient applied more than twice as much

Table 3.1. Pesticide use on all arable crop areas, percentage of actual crop area treated, and total quantities used on cereals in 1998. (Garthwaite and Thomas, 1999).

	Area[2] treated (ha x million)	% Area treated	Cereals (t active ingredient)
Insecticides + Nematicides	4.355	57.8	222
Fungicides	15.267	83.0	2629
Herbicides	13.979	93.8	6780
Molluscicides + repellents	0.537	7.7	95
Seed treatments	4.883	92.8	c100%

[2] *The area treated is the area x the number of treatments. On average 1 insecticide spray, 2 fungicide sprays and 2 herbicide sprays are applied to each crop. The figures include set-aside.*

herbicide is used as all the others together, partly because of the use of desiccants on potatoes. The balance of pesticide use in outdoor vegetables is rather different, with insecticides dominating, reflecting the importance of appearance in determining quality and value.

3.3. Types of pest

3.3.1. Weeds

It is virtually impossible directly to compare organic versus conventional treatment for specific 'pest' problems, but the experience of the CWS Focus on Farming Practice Organic Farming Experiments, 1989-1996 (Leake, 1996; Anon, 1996), is instructive. The crop protection summary states that "Pests and diseases have not significantly reduced yields over the period of the experiment and have generally occurred at lower levels than initially anticipated" but "Weeds have proved a major problem. Where fields had high populations of weeds at the conversion phase these have continued to be a problem and have reduced the profitability of these fields. Where weeds were at normal or low levels there has been no observable increase across the rotation, with the exception of certain perennial weeds".

All the evidence points to an increase in the weed seedbank in the soil during the conversion phase to organic production (Davies *et al*, 1997), and weeds are given as one of the main problems in organic vegetable production (Peacock and Norton, 1990). The methods used in organic systems (rotations, stale seed beds, seed rates, row spacing, hoeing, sowing date, flaming, intercropping and especially fertility building leys (see Greenland; Maxwell, this volume)) can, when properly applied, give adequate control of weeds but not to the same level as when herbicides are used (Moreby *et al*, 1994). The length of leys is also important with significantly better weed control when grass is down for more than two seasons (Davies *et al*, 1997, Younie *et al*, 1996), but for the stockless system the penalty resulting from taking land out of cash cropping for so long is prohibitive. The good news is, as the CWS results have tended to confirm, that the weed problem stabilises after a few years in an organic system.

Having more and a greater diversity of weeds, especially broad-leaved species (Moreby *et al*, 1994) is seen by the conventional farmer as a disadvantage. Some conventional farmers clearly adopt a zero-tolerance approach, on the grounds that any relaxation of weed control will build up problems for the future. The organic grower sees weeds, not only as competitors of the crop but also as sources of food for many parts of the food chain, the maintenance of which can make contributions to the minimisation of pest damage. In consequence an increase in weed diversity, provided crop production is not unduly compromised, is seen as acceptable (see Greenwood, this volume). However, one of the principal beneficiaries of such increased diversity is birds (see Greenwood, this volume) that some organic growers regard as important pests (Peacock and Norton, 1990).

Few farmers in conventional systems choose varieties on the basis of their competitiveness with weeds but it is clear that there are substantial differences between crops (Grundy *et al*, 1999, Wolfe, 2000) and within crop varieties

(Seavers and Wright, 1995). This is not surprising, but crop architecture has not featured greatly as a selection criterion for plant breeders although there has been much recent interest in the manipulation of crop canopy to restrict disease spread in wheat (Lovell *et al*, 1997).

The general consensus is that weeds are a greater problem in organic than conventional systems but the problems are not the same. For organic growers achieving a balance between weeds as competitors and constraints on crop yield and weeds as contributors to biodiversity will continue to be extremely difficult. For conventional growers whether or not to use new GM technology, that promises even more efficient weed control may well become the main decision to be made in future.

3.3.2. Invertebrates

Invertebrates in conventional farming are usually seen as feeding on the crop and thus removing resources that would otherwise be available to increase yield. In organic farming they are seen to have a dual role, both as potentially damaging but also as supplying food for other parts of the food chain or acting as predators on pests. This increased diversity is seen as helping to maintain a balance between beneficial and pest species and preventing the damaging outbreaks that are sometimes seen in conventionally-grown crops. A wide range of cultural methods are available to decrease pest problems and the associated viruses that many species, especially aphids transmit (Pimentel, 1993). Many of these methods e.g. rotations, intercropping, tillage, sowing dates, seed rates are common to all organic farming but newer methods that exploit behaviour are becoming increasingly available (Pickett *et al*, 1997; 1999) and have the potential to be very effective. There are also biological agents such as the Bt endotoxin that are approved for use as applications to organic crops, but not when expressed by the plant as a result of their incorporation in the plant's genome by genetic manipulation. However, biological control is rather little exploited in most outdoor crops (Langer, 1995) and is largely confined to crops grown where the conditions that are so critical for the effective deployment of biological agents can be controlled. On arable crops there are few invertebrates that appear to be serious constraints for organic growers, the exceptions being virus-transmitting aphids, which are usually avoided by manipulating drilling and planting dates, (e.g. autumn-sown cereals) or only grown where they are not a problem (seed potatoes). This is reflected in the relatively small use of insecticides on conventional arable crops (Table 3.1.). On vegetable crops where there is as much, if not more, emphasis on appearance as on yield, insect damage is a much greater problem and can be the reason why some crops are not grown by organic farmers in particular regions. Langer (1995) reported that the pest-sensitive cruciferous species such as radish, turnip and spring cabbage were often not grown because of cabbage root fly damage, and lettuces were seen as particularly prone to pest damage. Were this to continue, consumer choice could be restricted, if the aim is to source all temperate organic products from UK sources.

In both conventional and organic systems slugs are a serious problem, although generally more so in the winter-sown crops that are especially characteristic of conventional systems than in the spring-sown crops more often a feature of organic systems. However, the currently approved use of molluscicides in traps for organic crops expires within two years. While biological control agents for slugs are becoming available there is no obvious, acceptable economic replacement for slug control in arable crops for which large areas require treatment (Glen and Wilson, 1997).

In general, the organic grower does not see the pest role of invertebrates outweighing their role in natural control or their contribution to the wider food chain. While the occasional catastrophic loss to invertebrate pests might still occur, this seems no more likely than in conventional systems, and possibly less likely, because organic systems do appear to be more stable at a lower productivity level than conventionally-grown crops.

3.3.3. Diseases

All of the methods given above for mitigating the adverse effects of weeds and invertebrates can have similar benefits for diseases. Perhaps the most valuable is the use and choice of rotation to avoid the build up of soil-borne diseases or the accumulation of trash–borne inoculum and the most contentious is methods of tillage. The relative merits of ploughing versus minimum tillage need to be weighed carefully in the light of local problems, experience and crops.

Rotations will, however, provide little protection from diseases brought into the crop annually from large reservoirs of infection on other crops or species. Examples of such problems are powdery mildew and rusts on cereals and late blight on potatoes. For such problems novel approaches are necessary. Resistance is an important and effective method of control and many sources of resistance have been deployed in cereal breeding, although this approach has been less successful for potatoes. However, the pathogens have been adept at overcoming each newly introduced resistance. More durable resistance has been developed but each year there is an anxious wait to see if current resistance remains effective. The conventional monocropping system certainly encourages the development of pathogens capable of overcoming host resistance, and schemes have been devised to discourage growing varieties with the same or similar resistance characters near each other to disrupt the selection process (Anon, 2000).

A further development is growing mixtures of cultivars of the same species, or multilines, with contrasting resistance characteristics (Wolfe, 1985, Finckh and Wolfe, 1997; Finckh *et al*, 1999). This requires careful choice of varieties not only for their disease characteristics but also for other agronomic properties and has been extended on a more limited scale to mixtures of two species. The yield of the mean of the untreated mixtures is usually greater than the mean yield of the component varieties grown alone and untreated, and seems robust in the face of adverse conditions. Such schemes have been quite widely adopted in Eastern Europe and parts of North America, where they have also been deployed against soil-borne diseases (Finckh *et al*, 1999). Their disadvantage has been the current market requirement for single identified varieties, even if the varieties are subsequently blended before end use. If anything the market appears to be moving even further away from mixtures and even individual characteristics of feed varieties are being promoted. The effectiveness of mixtures has yet to be unequivocally demonstrated for crops other than cereals although it is being tested for the control of blight on potatoes. While organic growers can manipulate many crops effectively to minimise disease, and clearly benefit from the less liberal nitrogen nutrition available in organic crops, blight on potatoes remains a serious problem especially on maincrop varieties. This problem is likely to increase when copper is withdrawn as an acceptable fungicide in organic cropping. It is possible that as organic crop protection methods spread that there may be a decrease in the background level of pathogen inoculum and, in consequence, the current controls may be more effective with consequent benefits on yield. There is certainly some suggestion that yields do increase for a year or two following the conversion period of a single farm (Anon, 1996). However, there is an argument that because of the efficiency of conventional crop protection chemicals there is already a decrease in general inoculum which benefits the organic grower as much as the conventional farmer. However, for a disease such as blight on potatoes, the contamination of conventional crops that could result from uncontrolled blight on organic potato crops could become a serious problem (House of Lords, 1999).

Diseases seem likely to remain a serious potential constraint to yield of both conventional and organic crops. While appropriate rotations will largely prevent serious attacks of soil-borne disease in organic systems, annually introduced diseases will continue to restrict yield and in some crops pose a real threat of failure. Other husbandry methods being investigated and promoted such as mixed cropping of cereals and legumes (Clements *et al*, 1996) have uncertain effects but do appear to restrict the dispersal of some leaf diseases. Crop architecture, as for weed suppression, has also been intensively investigated both to help restrict disease development and the production of forecasting models (Lovell *et al*, 1997).

3.3.4. Crop seeds

Organic growers will soon be required to obtain their seeds from registered organic sources. This will pose a number of crop protection problems. Seed-borne diseases are common and can be extremely damaging; and they are rarely obvious from a quick examination. More than 90% of seed used in conventional agriculture is treated with pesticide (Table 3.1). While almost 50% of conventional arable farmers save their own seed they also have it treated. Organic growers, who especially favour home-saved seed, on the grounds that it is 'adapted' to local conditions, are at risk of perpetuating disease and suffering serious crop losses. It could also be argued that such crops could present an additional hazard to conventional farmers.

Another problem is the risk of weed contamination of seed. No weed control system should be undermined by the introduction of more weed seeds at sowing. Seed cleaning machinery can be very effective but adds cost and is rarely 100% efficient. It seems unlikely that sufficient seed can be produced within the UK for some time, especially in an expanding market and much will, in consequence, come from abroad with the attendant risks of introducing new weed and disease problems. This is not a problem exclusively for organic growers, but producing high quality organically sourced seed will be a real challenge over the next few years.

3.4. Diversity

Increasing or maintaining diversity is at the heart of the differences between conventional and organic agriculture and can be considered at several levels from plant to landscape. There is often an assumption that conventional agriculture tries to eliminate diversity to produce a monoculture of the desired species, the crop. However, the reality is rather different and surely only a minority of farmers seek to create a single species crop with no other species present, and certainly none succeed. Crop protection is based on establishing a balance between competing species, and decisions on whether or not to intervene are influenced by the likelihood of that balance favouring the desired species. Nowhere is this balance more important than in weed control, when the relative growth rate and growth characteristics of weed and crop are the basis of control decisions. Thus the critical concept for crop protection is that of thresholds (Anon, 1997), i.e. the level at which the effect of the pest on the crop can be economically prevented by the intervention of the grower, either by the use of a pesticide or by a method acceptable to organic standards. Thresholds will differ at different stages of growth, for different species and will critically depend on the factors that will influence the balance in the future between desired and unwanted species. The organic approach also stresses the benefits that some of these 'unwanted' species can bring, especially the diversity resulting from non-crop species either within or on the margins of the crop, which act as alternative food sources for pest species and as resources for beneficial invertebrates. Such benefits have been described as 'ecological' services. Thus conventional and organic farming should not be seen as incompatible, but as operating at different points along a continuum of activities.

The polarization of the debate about conventional and organic methods has led to the development and description of many 'middle-ground' systems described variously as lower-input or integrated. These have shown that large decreases in conventional inputs are possible while retaining acceptable yields and profitability (see Colman, this volume). Their economic success, or failure, depends not on the premia currently available to the organic grower, but on the cost of inputs decreasing more rapidly than the total value of the crop. Some of these systems are the way many farmers have been operating for many years. However, they have served to demonstrate that in many, but not all areas, pesticide inputs are in excess of those required by the threshold approach.

Trial and error was probably the biggest influence on how plant assemblages were first developed in agricultural environments. However, as our still limited understanding of the various interactions between all components of the environment improves, it should be possible to devise assemblages that deliver the desired 'ecological services', be it for the production of food or the creation of a particular wildlife habitat.

Changes in vegetation have an obvious impact beyond agriculture (see Greenwood, this volume) but changes in invertebrate populations are usually only recognised for a few visible groups, like butterflies and the interactions between various trophic levels associated with pest activity is rarely visible (Gange and Brown, 1997). Few would disagree that an increase in diversity is a 'good thing'. However, is an organic system necessary to provide that diversity and still retain effective crop protection? The basis of the LEAF approach, the FWAG and countryside stewardship schemes (see Tinker, this volume) is that conventional agriculture and biodiversity are not incompatible, and that biodiversity within a landscape need not compromise the crop, but does require a greater management input than 'easy' high input systems. The assumption is that it is possible to deliver high productivity and environmental quality using 'conventional' inputs, including crop protection chemicals. Such systems depend upon knowledge of the interactions between pests, the environment, and the crop and are often synonymous with Integrated Crop Protection or Integrated Crop Management. A real concern is that the organic approach is not taking advantage of all the opportunities there might be to maintain an effective and profitable UK agriculture within a diverse and valued environment. The description of 'ecological farming' does not seem to come with the same philosophical baggage as 'organic farming' but still may deliver the same advantages in environmental terms. Certainly there should be no prescription about what is acceptable; consumers should be given a choice.

The reality is that farming by its very nature sets out to favour one part of the biological community. Man does not differ from any other species in seeking to shape the world to his advantage. As Marsh (1995) has said... "if biological sustainability is conceived in terms of retaining all existing species, farming is an incompatible activity".

Past history is clearly a record of species loss and creation; species have adapted or expanded to fill the ecological niches left vacant. There seems no reason to assume that effective husbandry of the ecological resources with which farming works will not in the future ensure that the world's population receives food in the quantities and with the qualities that it desires. But the pressures on production as a result of population growth and the requirements of society will require that we make full use of all the environmental and technical resources available to us.

3.5. Concluding remarks

It is unfortunate that so much acrimonious debate has polarised views and attitudes concerning the relative merits or demerits of conventional and organic methods. Because there is a code and inspection system in place for organic agriculture it has an advantage over other systems, few of which are now as profligate with fertiliser and pesticide use as might be thought from the media. There is great enthusiasm and demand for organic food but the willingness of the consumer to pay a premium is vital. Others in this volume will discuss the safety of organic versus conventionally produced food but, while pesticides have caused illness and death, rarely, if ever, has this been through eating food correctly treated with them (Williams *et al*, this volume).

The organic system of crop protection requires different management skills from those required for conventional farming but the basis of all crop protection is knowledge of the interactions between crops and their environment. However, there is a trade-off of greater biodiversity against smaller yields in organic systems. It is good that there should be a choice for the consumer, provided that choice is guided by correct information. A mixed economy of food sources will be a feature of the future. As to the sustainability, or otherwise, of the various systems only time will tell. However, it seems unlikely that the lower productivity, higher prices and the rejection of advances in technology currently characteristic of organic agriculture, will be capable of feeding a world population of 9 billion by 2050 while retaining all the desired biodiversity and cherished landscapes, not only in the UK but throughout the world.

References

Anon. (1996) *Focus on Farming Practice. Organic Farming Experiments 1989-1996.* CWS Agriculture, Stoughton, Leicester.

Anon. (1997) *Private Costs and Benefits of Pesticide Minimisation.* Final Report. Risk and Policy Analysts Ltd. and Entec UK Ltd, Farthing Green House, 1 Beccles Road, Loddon, Norfolk pp 72 and Annexes.

Anon. (1999) *United Kingdom Register of Organic Food Standards (UKROFS)* Organic Farmers and Growers Standards for Organic Food Production. January 1999 Edition, Soham, Ely, Cambridgeshire.

Anon. (2000) *Cereals Variety Handbook.* National Institute of Agricultural Botany, Cambridge, UK.

Clements, R. O., Martyn, T.M., Balsdon, S., George, S. and Donaldson, G (1996) A clover:cereal bicropping system. In: *Aspects of Applied Biology 47: Rotations and Cropping Systems* (Eds. J. H. Clarke *et al*). Association of Applied Biologists, Wellesbourne, Warwick pp 185-194.

Davies, D. H. K., Christal, A., Talbot, M., Lawson, H.M. and Wright, G. McN. (1997) Changes in weed populations in the conversion of two arable farms to organic farming. *The 1997 Brighton Crop Protection Conference – Weeds.* The British Crop Protection Council, Farnham, Surrey pp 973-978

Finckh, M. R. and Wolfe, M. S. (1997) The use of biodiversity to restrict plant diseases and some consequences for farmers and society. In: *Ecology in Agriculture* (Ed. L. E. Jackson). Academic Press, London pp 203-237.

Finckh, M. R., Gacek, E. S., Czembor, H. J. and Wolfe, M. S. (1999) Host frequency and density effects on powdery mildew and yield in mixtures of barley cultivars. *Plant Pathology,* **48**, 807-816.

Gange, A. C. and Brown, V. K.(Eds) (1997) *Multitrophic Interactions in Terrestrial Ecosystems.* 36th Symposium of the British Ecological Society, Blackwell Science, Oxford pp 448.

Garthwaite, D. G. and Thomas, M. R. (1999) *Pesticide Usage Survey Report 159. Arable Farm Crops in Great Britain 1998.* Pesticide Usage Survey Group, Central Science Laboratory, York pp 97.

Glen, D. M. and Wilson, M. J. (1997) Slug-parasitic nematodes as biocontrol agents for slugs. *Agro-Food-Industry Hi-Tech* **8**, 23-27.

Grundy, A. C., Bond, W., Burston, S. and Jackson, L. (1999) *Weed suppression by crops. The 1999 Brighton Conference- Weeds.* The British Crop Protection Council, Farnham, Surrey pp 957-962.

House of Lords (1999) House of Lords Select Committee on European Communities Report (16th Report). *Organic farming and the European Union.* Stationery Office, London.

Jenkyn, J. F. and Bainbridge, A. (1978) Biology and Pathology of Cereal Powdery Mildews. In: *The Powdery Mildews* (Ed. D. Spencer). Academic Press, London pp 284-321.

Lampkin, N. and Measures, M. (1999) *Organic Farm Management Handbook.* Organic Farming Unit, University of Wales, Aberystwyth, and Organic Advisory Service, Elm Farm Research Centre, Newbury, UK pp 163.

Langer, V. (1995) Pests and Diseases in organically grown vegetables in Denmark: a survey of problems and use of control measures. *Biological Agriculture and Horticulture,* **12** 151-171.

Leake, A. R. (1996) The effect of cropping systems and rotational management: An economic comparison of conventional, integrated and organic systems. In: *Aspects of Applied Biology, 47: Rotations and Cropping Systems* (Eds. J. H. Clarke *et al*). Association of Applied Biologists, Wellesbourne, Warwick pp 185-194.

Lovell, D. J., Parker, S. R., Hunter, T., Royle, D. J. and Coker, R. R. (1997) Influence of crop growth and structure on the risk of epidemics by *Mycosphaerella graminicola (Septoria tritici)* in winter wheat. *Plant Pathology*, **46**, 126-138.

Marsh J. S. (1995) The policy approach to sustainable farming systems in the EU. In: *British Crop Protection Council Symposium 63, Integrated Crop Protection: Towards Sustainability*. British Crop Protection Council, Farnham, Surrey pp 13-23.

Metcalf, R. L. (1986) The ecology of insecticides and the chemical control of insects. In: *Ecological Theory and Integrated Pest Management Practice* (Ed. M. Kogan). John Wiley, New York pp 251-297.

Moreby, S. J., Aebischer, N.J., Southway, S. E. and Sotherton, N. W. (1994) A comparison of the flora and arthropod fauna of organically and conventionally grown winter wheat in southern England. *Annals of Applied Biology*, **125**, 13-27

Peacock, L. and Norton, G. A. (1990) A critical analysis of organic vegetable crop protection in the UK. *Agriculture, Ecosystems and Environment*, **31**, 187-197

Pickett, J. A., Wadhams, L.J. and Woodcock, C. M. (1997) Developing sustainable pest control from chemical ecology. *Agriculture, Ecosystems and Environment, 12*, 149-156

Pickett, J. A., Chamberlain, K., Poppy, G. M. and Woodcock, C. M. (1999) Exploiting insect responses in identifying plant signals. In: *Insect-Plant Interactions and Induced Plant Defence, Novartis Foundation Symposium 223* (Ed. J. Goode). John Wiley, Chichester pp 253-265.

Pimentel, D. (1993) Cultural Control for Insect Pest Management. In: *Pest Control and Sustainable Agriculture* (Eds. S. Corey, D, Dall and W. Milne). CSIRO Australia pp 35-38.

Seavers, G. P. and Wright, K.J. (1995) Potential for weed control by suppressive cereal cultivars. In: *Proceedings British Crop Protection Council, Weeds, Brighton November, 1995*. BCPC, Farnham, Surrey pp 737-742.

Wolfe, M. S. (1985) The current status and prospects of multiline cultivars and variety mixtures for disease resistance. *Annual Review of Phytopathology*, **23**, 251-273

Wolfe, M. S. (2000) EFRC Cereal Trials 2000. *Elm Farm Research Centre Bulletin*, July, 2000 p11.

Younie, D., Watson, Christine A and Squire, G. R. (1996) A comparison of crop rotations in organic farming: agronomic performance. In: *Aspects of Applied Biology 47, Rotations and Cropping Systems* (Eds. J. H. Clarke *et al*). Association of Applied Biologists, Wellesbourne, Warwick 379-382.

Chapter Four

Livestock Systems and Animal Husbandry

Professor T J Maxwell OBE, BSc, PhD, FRSGS, FRSE, CBiol, FIBiol, ARAgS
Dr P J Goddard BVetMed, PhD, MRCVS

4.1. Introduction

Recent outbreaks of food poisoning and the occurrence of BSE have led to an increasing concern about the safety and quality of livestock products. The animal husbandry associated with intensive livestock production, for example the use of growth promoters, antibiotics, processed offal in livestock feed, high density housing, poor animal welfare and lack of hygiene are aspects of livestock management that have contributed to these concerns (see Williams *et al*, this volume).

The industry has responded in several ways. Most conventional livestock farmers have recognised the urgency of introducing quality assurance schemes and stringent welfare standards as means of raising consumer confidence (Wood *et al*, 1998). This includes intensive livestock farmers who continue to rely heavily on prophylactic health programmes to maintain high levels of output. Others, while adopting quality assurance and stringent standards have integrated their livestock and/or crop production systems within the concepts of 'less intensive farming for the environment' – LIFE projects or 'linking environment with farming' – LEAF projects. But organic livestock farmers adhere to a much stricter and holistic code of practice. This includes livestock production from grassland, in which the role of animals in the production of organic manure is an integral component of organic farming.

Attempting to evaluate the extent to which stringent organic regulations provide additional benefits with respect to the management of grassland, and its impact on animal nutrition and the environment is important for two reasons. First, the levels of output from organic systems are lower than those from conventional systems (Younie and Hermansen, 2000) and therefore organic products are sold at a higher price; secondly, any increase in demand in the long run will require consumers to be convinced that the additional benefits justify their additional cost (see Tinker, this volume).

4.2. Grassland in livestock systems

Efficient grassland production and utilisation are central to successful conventional and intensive ruminant livestock agriculture in the United Kingdom. High levels of output have been achieved because of improvements in the persistence and yield of grass and clover species. The use of nitrogen, phosphorus, potassium and other fertilisers has further enhanced the ability to vary the distribution of yield, and high stocking rates and high levels of meat and/or milk output per unit area have been achieved. Most livestock grassland farmers have also adopted systems of management that control and reduce parasitic infections and nutrient deficiencies, using reduced stocking densities, 'clean' grazing systems, strategic anthelmintic dosing and provision of feed supplements at crucial periods of the year. All grassland farmers attempt to maximise the use of grass through a controlled allocation of grassland for grazing and the production of hay and silage for winter feed.

Organic ruminant stock must have access to pasture during the growing season, and throughout the year must be fed a diet that is at least 60% green forage, on a daily dry matter basis. 'Organic' animals must not be kept on non-organic land at any time and conventional fertilisers cannot be used. A minimum of 80-90% of feed must come from organic sources (see Greenland, this volume) depending on the category of stock and certifying body concerned. Little comparative information is available on the impact of these requirements on the nutrition of organic livestock. But there is no apparent reason why significant differences should occur between an organic and conventional diet of similar composition. However, it does appear that metabolic disorders are at a relatively low level on organic dairy farms. One explanation for this may be a less intensive level of production (Boehncke, 1998) associated with a reliance on high quality, home-produced fodder and less concentrates.

4.2.1. Nitrogen economy

Efficient grassland management is synonymous with the efficient management of nutrients, especially nitrogen. Much nitrogen can be lost from grassland systems by leaching if fertiliser applications exceed the capacity of the crop to assimilate the amounts applied. It is therefore crucial that the seasonal application of nitrogen fertiliser matches the growth potential of the grass or grass/clover pasture.

Pastures with similar stock carrying capacity produce similar losses of N, regardless of whether the N is derived from N-fixation by legumes or supplied by fertiliser N (Titchen and Philipps, 1996). However, a number of comparative studies have shown that normally there is less N leached from clover-based systems, including organic grassland than from intensively fertilised grassland (Halberg *et al*, 1995; Watson and Younie, 1995). This reflects the differences in the amount of nitrogen cycling within the different systems and Halberg *et al* (1995) have suggested that substantial reductions in nitrogen loss from conventional mixed dairy farms must imply lower production. Younie and Hermansen (2000) have pointed out, however, that the most crucial point for N leaching is in the transition from ley to arable cropping and that autumn ploughing leads to more leaching than spring ploughing in all systems with rotational grassland.

There is, however an inevitable mismatch between optimising nitrogen for grass growth and the grazing ruminant. The concentration of crude protein in grass often exceeds a ruminant's requirements, particularly in the spring and early summer, and results in the excretion of excess nitrogen which is leached or volatilised as ammonia into the atmosphere. There appears to be no difference between conventional and organic systems. Halberg *et al* (1995) estimated ammonia losses from organic dairy farms in Denmark to vary over the same range as conventional farms, although stocking rates tended to be lower than on conventional farms. Similarly, there appear to be no differences in the greenhouse gases produced by organic and conventional dairy systems, so the amount of carbon dioxide equivalent per unit of milk produced is almost identical (Bakken *et al*, 1994).

With respect to species diversity, the evidence that organic grass/clover permanent pastures are more diverse in their botanical composition than conventional grass/clover pastures seems to be equivocal (Younie and Hermansen, 2000).

White clover is by far the best of the legumes for UK grazing conditions in terms of yield, persistence and N-fixing capability. It is also of high nutritive value. Perennial ryegrass is also the most suitable species for ley farming in the UK; it is easy to establish, has a high yield potential of high nutritional value, and is persistent. It is also a good companion grass to white clover. This is recognised by conventional as well as organic farmers. Nitrogen is an essential nutrient for herbage growth in all grassland livestock systems, but in organic systems its supply is dependent upon N from the atmosphere and rain (20-30 kg/ha), the mineralisation of organic N and the fixation of atmospheric N by legumes, particularly white clover.

For organic systems, it is argued that as the build up of 'fixed-N' in the organic matter increases in the soil, an increasing proportion of the N is supplied from mineralised organic N with a relatively lower contribution coming from current N fixation. However, this is not possible without a net decrease in soil organic N. Kristensen *et al* (1995) calculated that after correcting for differences in climate, the 'organic' yield of grass/clover swards was 12-14% lower than from conventional systems. In order to compensate for such differences the Danish Central Advisory Service (1998) calculate that an organic premium of 15-20% is necessary for organic milk production to maintain a level of profit equivalent to conventional milk production. In Denmark, from 1993-1997, the organic milk price at the farm gate was 30-40% higher than the conventional milk price!

4.2.2. Potassium and phosphorus

Younie and Hermansen (2000) emphasised the importance of maintaining soil potassium and phosphorus status on organic livestock farms. The removal of nutrients from fields cut for hay or silage will reduce soil K and P content and consequently herbage and crop yield, though its extent will depend upon soil type. Fothergill *et al* (1995) showed the adverse effects of low P and K soil status on clover content and consequently on N fixation in upland pasture. They note that even if 100% efficiency in internal nutrient cycling were possible, there would still be a considerable loss of P and K in crop and livestock products sold off the farm and in leaching losses in the field (Nolte and Werner, 1994; see Greenland this volume). Younie and Hermansen (2000) stress the priority of giving manure to grass/clover swards intended for conservation, particularly on sandy soils.

Animal manure contains some 4g N, 2g P and 2.5g K per kg (Whittemore, 1995). If a reduction in nutrients in herbage occurs because the frequency and/ or amounts are reduced within organic farming systems, there may be a need to supply nutritional supplements, particularly phosphorus and in many pastoral systems magnesium (Hemmingway, 1999) during periods of rapid grass growth.

In organic systems these nutritional deficiencies may not appear immediately since there is likely to be a surplus of many of these nutrients as a result of previous fertiliser practices. Clearly farmers adopting a low or nil fertiliser manure policy will need to be particularly vigilant in identifying any symptoms of nutrient deficiencies in their stock.

A more conventional grassland management approach, using modest levels of conventional fertiliser can alleviate these problems, while retaining the clover content of the pastures and all the other essential elements of efficient grassland management. The restriction on organic livestock farmers applying modest levels of chemical fertilisers is a significant penalty that they must recoup from higher product prices.

4.3. Animal health and welfare

It is self-evident that animal health is much more than the simple absence of disease; it has to include aspects of housing, welfare, and the appropriate choice of breeds and species that are adapted to different systems of livestock management. Sympathetic husbandry methods are regarded as the first line of defence against ill health in organic livestock systems. Routine prophylactic use of drugs is not allowed. There is a ban on feeds containing growth promoters, antibiotics, solvent extracted ingredients and genetically modified organisms. Although conventional medicines may be used for animals showing clinical signs of disease, animals so treated may then be affected by an extended withdrawal period – the period between last use of a medicine and the sale of an animal product for human consumption. Treatment to alleviate suffering, however, must never be withheld. Organic livestock farmers are required to develop a plan to ensure health building and to introduce disease control measures that lead progressively to less dependence upon conventional medicines. But health plans form part of most conventional livestock management and farm assurance schemes. UKROFS suggests that high quality feed, regular exercise and access to pasture encourage the natural immunological defence of the animal; this needs to be justified, though few would dispute that the provision of these needs accords with best practice and good standards of animal welfare.

4.3.1. Housing and general welfare issues
Housing and social groupings which take account of established ethological criteria are important aspects of many modern production systems, and the organic standards include these. The most significant advances have been made regarding pigs and poultry. Some relatively straightforward changes (such as the increased use of bedding materials) are very advantageous. However, these are not solely issues for organic producers. The development of animal welfare indices, based on components such as freedom of movement, social interaction, condition of flooring, light, ventilation and quality of care (Schmid, 1998) are equally applicable to conventional farming systems. While the move towards more extensive production systems may have ethological advantages for the animals concerned, there are also implications for management. One particular problem for those keeping sheep in extensive hill environments is the Soil

Association's requirement that those using rubber rings for castration or docking of lambs must apply them within 72 hours of birth, with no recommendation for a method to use thereafter until the lambs are 3 weeks old, when a knife or hot iron can be used. Similarly, some activities currently practised to facilitate the management of cattle (e.g. castration, disbudding of calves) must not be undertaken routinely, but can only be carried out if they are intended to improve the health, welfare or hygiene of the livestock.

The behavioural needs of all the species we use in agriculture are not precisely known, but the general principle is that breeds of animals should be chosen that are suited to the production system used. For example, in intensive pig production systems it is important to avoid the use of breeds or strains of pig that are susceptible to specific diseases or health problems (e.g. porcine stress syndrome). It is notable that organic livestock producers tend to give preference to indigenous breeds or strains well adapted to their production environment.

Lameness may differ in incidence with organic management. Since diseases of the foot constitute one of the most common on-farm problems and result in poor animal performance, it is important to establish effective methods of control. While there have been reports of a lower incidence of lameness amongst dairy cows on organic farms (Esslemont and Spincer, 1993; Offerhaus *et al*, 1994), many factors, possibly directly or indirectly related to organic methods may be responsible as there are often large between-farm differences (Weller and Cooper, 1996).

Overall, while organic farmers *must* adhere to relevant standards, many conventional producers, particularly those subscribing to a range of farm assurance schemes, adopt quite similar methods. This applies especially to those engaged upon more extensive systems of production. Therefore in practice there may be little to distinguish between production systems.

4.3.2. Preventive medicine

UKROFS principles tend to eschew the use of conventional medicines, yet the efficacy of phytotherapeutic or homeopathic products is uncertain. Vaccination is restricted to cases where there is a known disease risk. Pre-emptive treatment against parasites, which many consider to be a crucial component of preventive medicine strategies, is also restricted. From an animal welfare perspective, preventing a disease which is likely to occur is more acceptable than responding to disease in affected animals. However, Krutzinna *et al* (1996b) reported that the health status of organic dairy cows seemed not to differ fundamentally from that of conventional herds, and Roderick *et al* (1996) noted that without a comparative epidemiological study it was not clear whether disease levels differed between conventional and organic farms. The comparative advantage of organic farming in disease control has yet to be unequivocally demonstrated. It is therefore difficult to accept the general presumption against the pre-emptive use of preventive medicine for organic livestock, and that it has a beneficial effect on the 'organic' status of products.

4.3.2.1. Parasite control
The control of internal and external parasites is one of the most important preventive measures of livestock farmers. A low stocking rate will most likely

reduce the importance of nematode infections or nematode-associated health problems, although lungworm disease remains a recurrent problem. However, the interplay between nematode populations, pasture and animals is very complex. There will also be an impact of nutrition on animal immunity, and so even at low stocking rates, nematodes may still constitute a problem for stock if the plane of nutrition is low (Thamsborg, 1998). There is growing evidence of parasite resistance to a number of important, widely used anthelmintics (Jackson and Coop, 1994; Stafford and Coles, 1999), promoting the need to develop strategies for parasite control which go beyond the simple use of these compounds. In the future it may be possible to develop integrated control methods based on clean grazing and biological control, though at present grazing management is the only method to avoid the substantial use of anthelmintics (Thamsborg *et al*, 1999). However, some parasites may exhibit significant persistence on pasture, even in the absence of the primary host (Coop *et al*, 1991). Organic standards allow for the use of anthelmintics therapeutically so that the presence of unacceptable worm burdens can be eliminated, but thereafter conventional preventive treatment is not allowed. Clearly, in these circumstances the development of effective vaccines against parasites (Lawrence *et al*, 1996) would be helpful. Keatinge (1996) noted that to be successful current systems of clean grazing still depend upon strategically-timed anthelmintic treatment and that the best prospect for parasite control is to combine several approaches in an integrated control programme. For organic farms supporting "commercial" stocking rates, limited use of anthelmintics is almost inevitable (Keatinge, 1996).

It may be possible to breed sheep and goats with greater resistance to parasitic infection. Conventional selection programmes have demonstrated that host resistance can be improved in goats: Coop (personal communication) has demonstrated a reduction in parasitic egg counts of 33% after five generations of breeding for resistance. Such an approach is very relevant to organic producers, but is equally important to all livestock producers where there is increasing parasitic resistance to anthelmintics.

4.3.2.2. Treatment of mastitis

The situation regarding the incidence and severity of mastitis on organic dairy farms is unclear. Even in ecologically managed dairy farms mastitis remains the main disease entity (Fehlings and Deneke, 2000) and strict hygiene and prophylactic treatment remain important. While it is difficult to establish good control data, it would appear that on some organic dairy farms the incidence of mastitis during the dry period may be of particular concern (Weller and Bowling, 2000). In Germany, Krutzinna *et al* (1996a) reported serious health problems of the udder.

The prophylactic use of antibiotics to prevent mastitis occurring during the non-lactating period on a herd basis is prohibited on organic farms. Boehncke (1998) noted that while homeopathy may be as successful as antibiotics in the treatment of mastitis, its application does require considerable experience. Myllys *et al* (1994) made the interesting comment that essentially the use of antibiotics for decades has altered the bacterial ecology of the udder rather than eliminated infection. Overall milk production will depend upon the quality of management, whatever the system. But again breeding programmes that select against a high incidence of mastitis will in the long term secure a more satisfactory set of circumstances for the organic farmer as well as the conventional farmer. Whether this can be achieved more easily when cows are managed less intensively, as in an organic system, remains to be established.

4.3.3. Use of antibiotics

The appearance in human pathogens of multiple resistance to antibiotics has focused attention on the use of antibiotics in both animals and man (FVE, 1999). There appears little doubt that the use of antibiotics in animal production is contributing to the difficulties encountered in the use of antibiotics to treat humans (Knudtson and Hartman, 1993). Though the direct use of antibiotics in humans is probably having a greater effect than that attributable to animal use, the responsible and prudent use of antibiotics in animals is essential, regardless of the production system (ACMSF, 1999). It has been suggested that special attention should be paid to the veterinary use of the fluoroquinolone family of antibiotics since these have a particular benefit to humans in their ability to be used against some resistant bacteria. Thus there is a growing consensus that a change in the use of antibiotics in the rearing of food animals is now necessary and possible and the promotion of a reduction in antibiotic use by the organic movement is constructive and helpful.

A second issue relates to the presence of antibiotic residues in animal products. It is not clear why proposals regarding withdrawal periods for veterinary medicines have been set by UKROFS at double the official requirement.

4.3.4. Antibiotics used as growth promoters

It is well known that antibiotics are given to animals as growth promoters. However, the Soil Association report on the use of antibiotics in UK agriculture (Harvey and Mason, 1998) raised the interesting point that withdrawal of some currently used growth-promoting antibiotics may lead to an increase in the use of therapeutic antibiotics to bridge the gap created in disease control. Whatever the farming system, an accurate assessment of the risk/benefit of the use of antimicrobial agents is increasingly desirable and would provide useful data, even if such an analysis still leaves the ethical question as to what is considered acceptable practice to be answered.

The Soil Association is calling for a ban on all non-medicinal use of antibiotics in agriculture. Clearly there are widespread concerns about the consequences for both human and animal health of the use of antibiotics in this role and a ban on the use of four growth promoters (bacitracin zinc, spiramycin, tylosin phosphate and virginiamycin) was introduced in 1999 following a ban on the use of avoparcin in 1997. A working group, under the auspices of the Advisory Committee on the Microbial Safety of Food, was established to assess the risk to humans from antibiotic resistant micro-organisms entering the food chain. The group considered the need for any action to protect public health and reported in 1999, with numerous recommendations (ACMSF, 1999). These included constraining the use of growth promoters, developing strategies for reducing the use of antibiotics for therapy and prophylaxis, the introduction of tighter controls on medicated feedstuffs, and enhanced training for those involved in the supply and use of antibiotics, together with a number of strategic research recommendations.

4.4. The impact of livestock farming on different farming systems

Mixed farming, (i.e. livestock grassland farming as an integral part of an arable crop rotation), was the accepted mode of farming on much of the land suitable for arable cropping in the UK until the relatively recent era of specialisation. It was then largely abandoned until the recent movement towards the adoption of more environmentally friendly farming methods and the Government's introduction of financial support for conversion to organic farming. This has encouraged some specialist livestock rearing and dairy farmers to enter organic conversion schemes and meet the growing demand for organic livestock products.

While there is evidence to support the inclusion of grassland and the application of manure as part of an arable rotation in maintaining soil structure and organic matter, without inorganic fertilisers yields both of grassland and arable crops are not as high as in conventional or integrated farming. While there is evidence that organic cropping can be as profitable as conventional cropping this is not so apparent with respect to the livestock sector (see Colman, this volume). However, the inclusion of grassland livestock and the production and application of organic manure in integrated and organic systems clearly have merit in contributing to more environmentally enhancing and benign methods of farming (see Greenwood, this volume).

The overall conclusion on the limited and variable evidence available is that environmental pollution from grassland livestock production is related to stocking rate. Therefore, integrated and organic systems, which operate at lower stocking rates, create less pollution per unit area than conventional systems. While there are clearly benefits to the environment by lowering the intensity of livestock production, there are clear implications for profitability and size of operation. An area farmed organically will have to be greater to return the same level of income as that obtained from a smaller area of land conventionally farmed. Alternatively the organic premium will have to remain significantly greater if organic livestock farming is to survive without continuing financial support from government after conversion. However, this may in itself be justified on environmental grounds alone.

But it is also important that if the demand for organic products is to grow, the discerning consumer will need to be convinced that their higher cost is matched by additional benefits. Yet relatively little rigorous information exists regarding the comparative quality of organic, compared to conventional, livestock products (see Williams *et al*, this volume). Honikel (1998) has suggested that the characteristics of quality of animal products, (i.e. the nutritional, hygienic and sensory properties) were not very different between organic and conventional production; but clearly the production system itself has a value to those consumers who purchase organic products.

There can be little doubt that since the BSE crisis livestock producers have become much more vigilant in their approach to hygiene, animal welfare and the sources of the feed they use for their stock. Additionally they are also conscious of the need to adopt cost effective programmes of health care. It is in this area that there is currently a significant contrast in management between conventional and organic livestock producers. There seems to be good reason to reduce the use of antibiotics across all systems of production in the interests of the animals themselves as well as the potential effect on humans. The case for not allowing other conventional preventive medicine approaches, such as the strategic use of anthelminitics in the control of parasites, is less convincing.

References

Advisory Committee on the Microbiological Safety of Food (ACMSF) (1999) *Report on microbial antibiotic resistance relating to food safety.* The Stationery Office, London, 320 pp.

Bakken, L., Refsgaard, K., Christensen, S. and Vatn, A. (1994) Energy use and emission of greenhouse gases from grassland agricultural systems. In: *Grassland and Society* (Eds. L. 't Mannetje, and J. Frame). Proceedings, 15th General Meeting, European Grassland Federation, Wageningen, 361-376.

Boehncke, E. (1998) Animal health and welfare aspects of organic systems. In: *The implications of extensification for the health and welfare of beef cattle and sheep* (Ed. P.J. Goddard). Proceedings of a workshop held in Aberdeen, Scotland. MLURI, Aberdeen, 59-61.

Coop, R.L., Jackson, F. and Jackson, E. (1991) Relative contribution of cattle to contamination of pasture with *Nematodirus battus* under field conditions. *Research in Veterinary Science*, **50**, 211-215.

Danish Central Advisory Service (1998) *Production-economy-ecology* (in Danish). DCAS, Denmark pp 15.

Esslemont, R.J. and Spincer, I. (1993) The incidence and costs of disease in dairy herds. *Dairy Information System Report No. 2*, University of Reading.

Fehlings, K. and Deneke, J. (2000) Mastitis in ecologically managed dairy farms. *Tierarztliche Praxis*, **28**, 104-109.

Fothergill, M., Davies, D.A. and Morgan, C.T. (1995) The effect of extensification of upland pastures on white clover. In: *Grassland into the 21st Century – Occasional Symposium*, (Ed. G.E. Pollott). No 29 British Grassland Society, Reading, 171-172.

FVE (1999) *Antibiotic resistance and prudent use of antibiotics in veterinary medicine.* Federation of Veterinarians of Europe, Brussels pp 12.

Halberg, N., Kristense, E.S. and Kristensen, I.S. (1995) Nitrogen turnover on organic and conventional mixed farms. *Journal of Agricultural and Environmental Ethics*, **8**, 30-51.

Harvey, J. and Mason, L. (1998) *The use and misuse of antibiotics in UK agriculture. Part 1: Current usage.* Soil Association, Bristol, UK, pp 39.

Hemmingway, R.G. (1999) The effect of changing patterns of fertilizer applications on the major mineral composition of herbage in relation to requirements of cattle: a 50-year review. *Animal Science*, **69**, 1-18.

Honikel, K.O. (1998) Quality of ecologically produced foods of animal origin. *Deutsche Tierarztliche Wochenschrift*, **105**, 327-329.

Jackson, F. and Coop, R.L. (1994) Anthelmintic resistant roundworms in sheep and goats. *The Moredun Foundation Newsheet*, 2, No. 3. April, 1994.

Keatinge, R. (1996) *Controlling internal parasites without anthelmintics (A review).* Report prepared for MAFF, ADAS Redesdale, Newcastle-upon-Tyne. pp 75.

Kristensen, E.S., Hogh-Jensen, H., and Kirstensen, I.S. (1995) A simple model for the estimation of atmospherically-derived nitrogen in grass-clover systems. *Biological Agriculture and Horticulture*, *12*, 263-276.

Knudtson, L.M. and Hartman, P.A. (1993) Antibiotic resistance among enterococcal isolates from environmental and clinical sources. *Journal of Food Protection*, **56**, 489-492.

Krutzinna, C., Boehncke, E. and Herrmann, H.J. (1996a) Organic milk production in Germany. *Biological Agriculture and Horticulture*, **13**, 351-358.

Krutzinna, C., Boehncke, E. and Herrmann, H.J. (1996b) Organic dairy husbandry. *Berichte uber Landwirtschaft*, **74**, 461-480.

Lawrence, S.B., Heath, D.D., Harrison, G.B.L., Robinson, C.M., Dempster, R.P., Gatehouse, T.K., Lightowlers, M.W. and Rickard, M.D. (1996) Pilot field trial of a recombinant Taenia ovis vaccine in lambs exposed to natural infection. *New Zealand Veterinary Journal*, **44**, 155-157.

Myllys, V., Honkanen-Buzalski, T., Houvinen, P., Sandholm, M. and Nurmi, E. (1994) Association of changes in bacterial ecology of bovine mastitis with changes in the use of milking machines and antibacterial drugs. *Acta veterinaria Scandinavica*, **35**, 363-369.

Nolte, C. and Werner, W. (1994) Investigations on the nutrient cycle and its components of a biodynamically-managed farm. *Biological Agriculture and Horticulture, 10*, 235-254.

Offerhaus, E.J., Baars, T. and Grommers, F.J. (1994) *Gezondheid en vruchtbaarheid van melkvee op biologische bedrijven*. Luis Bolk Institute, Driebergen.

Roderick, S., Short, N. and Hovi, M. (1996) *Organic livestock production: Animal health and welfare research priorities*. University of Reading.

Schmid, E. (1998) Minimum care for maximum welfare. In: *The implications of extensification for the health and welfare of beef cattle and sheep* (Ed. P.J.Goddard). Proceedings of a workshop held in Aberdeen, Scotland. MLURI, Aberdeen, 71-74.

Stafford, K. and Coles, G.C. (1999) Nematode control practices and anthelmintic resistance in dairy calves in the south west of England. *Veterinary Record*, **144**, 659-661.

Thamsborg, S.M. (1998) Implications of extensification for endoparasitic infections. In: *The implications of extensification for the health and welfare of beef cattle and sheep* (Ed. P.J.Goddard). Proceedings of a workshop held in Aberdeen, Scotland. MLURI, Aberdeen, 63-69.

Thamsborg, S.M., Roepstorff, A. and Larsen, M. (1999) Integrated and biological control of parasites in organic and conventional production systems. *Veterinary Parasitology*, **84**, 169-186.

Titchen, N.M. and Philipps, L. (1996) Environmental effects of legume based grassland systems. In: *Legumes in Sustainable Farming Systems. Occasional Symposium No 30* (Ed. D. Younie). British Grassland Society, Reading, 257-261.

Watson, C.A. and Younie, D. (1995) Nitrogen balances in organically and conventionally managed beef production systems. In: *Grassland into the 21st Century. Occasional Symposium No29* (Ed G.E. Pollott). British Grassland Society, Reading, 197-199.

Weller, C.A. and Bowling, P.J. (2000) Health status of dairy herds in organic farming. *Veterinary Record*, **146**, 141-142.

Weller, R.F. and Cooper, A. (1996) Health status of dairy herds converting from conventional to organic dairy farming. *Veterinary Record*, **139**, 141-142.

Whittemore, C.T. (1995) Animal excreta: fertilizer or pollutant? *Journal of Biological Education*, **29**, 46-50.

Wood, J.D., Holder, J.S. and Main, D.C.J. (1998) Quality assurance schemes. *Meat Science*, **49**, S191-S203.

Younie, D. and Hermansen, J. (2000) The role of grassland in organic livestock farming. *Grassland Science in Europe, 5*, 493-509.

Chapter Five

Comparative Economics of Farming Systems

Professor D R Colman BSc, MS, PhD

5.1. Introduction

The primary aim of this chapter will be to consider evidence concerning the relative profitability of organic and "conventional" agricultural production in the UK and the role of premium prices for organic produce. There are a number of other economic issues which will be touched upon. The chapter will briefly review the growth of the market for organic products. It will also consider the question of subsidies for organic farming, since the UK has a different policy to most other EU states. There is also the question of the economics of "intermediate" farming systems which do not qualify for organic status, but which nevertheless are committed to some of the practices and ideals of organic farmers.

5.2. Growth of the UK organic sector

5.2.1. Organic demand

The UK market for certified organic food is expanding rapidly, although its size in terms of share of total food expenditure lags significantly behind that in other EU member states, most notably Austria, Switzerland, Sweden, Finland, Germany, Italy, and Denmark.

In 1997 the retail value of organic food sales in the UK was estimated at £260 million. Of this fruit and vegetables accounted for 54%, cereals 14%, dairy products 7% and meats 4%. A summary of the estimated position in 1997 is provided by Michelson *et al* (1999), and reproduced as Table 5.1.

The rate of market growth is very high, and from 1997 to 1998/9 its retail value is estimated to have risen by 50% to £390 million (Soil Association, 1999). Nevertheless the basic picture in Table 5.1 has been maintained, after allowing

Table 5.1. The UK market for the most important organic food products, 1997 (Michelson *et al*, 1999)

Product group	Market share of organics (%)	Organic share imported (%)
Vegetables	2.3	70
Fruits (inc. nuts)	1.0	90
Potatoes	0.6	60
Milk products	0.35	12
Meats	no data	3
Cereals	0.2	15

for the resultant growth in organic produce's share of the market. A high proportion of the UK market is supplied by imports as UK organic food supply growth has lagged behind demand growth. Import penetration is particularly high in vegetables and fruit where organic products exhibit very high price premia, and the share of imports has continued to grow since 1997.

At present total organic demand accounts for a small proportion of the total food market, but with growth projected at 40% per annum by the Soil Association (SA, 1999, p.22) it might reach 8% of the market within five years. If demand continues to expand at this sort of rate, a greater share of the market is captured by UK producers, and the price difference over non-organic produce is maintained, the prospects for output by UK organic producers to expand are good. In the immediate future demand growth will be aided by reductions in the retail level organic premium without comparable erosion in the prices paid to organic producers.

Organic foods currently command significantly higher prices than the average of non-organic foods at both consumer and producer levels, but this is more marked for vegetables than it is for livestock products. These higher prices reflect the willingness of a growing number of consumers to pay for the perceived characteristics of organic food. Such perceptions, and the price premia which they command, are also shared to some extent by food products which may not be classified organic, but which can be marketed under a label which identifies preferred qualities in the production system and which additionally may be interpreted as being reflected in improved food safety and nutritional quality. The certified organic label is only a guarantee that certain production methods have been used (and more importantly that others have been avoided), and it is these which consumers are increasingly willing to pay for. The superior nutritional characteristics assumed to follow from these are however less strongly apparent, and organic certification is not a guarantee of specific nutritional properties. There is little convincing evidence that the nutritional properties of organic foods are necessarily higher than uncertified products (McKerron *et al*, 1999 p.63; Williams *et al*, this volume).

5.2.2. UK organic farming supply

According to the SA (1999) by April 1999 the UK area of land that was fully organic was 60,000 hectares and the amount in conversion was 180,000. This total of 240,000 is equivalent to 1.3% of the UK's Utilisable Agricultural Area, a share which has increased by 384% since 1995. Of the organic land in 1999, 21% was being used for cropping, of which approximately 9,650 ha was for combinable crops and 3,000 ha. was for fruit and vegetable production. The remaining 79% of the land was under grass, and legume crops for green manure. A high proportion of the grassland (over 105,000 ha.) is classed as rough grazing and is used for extensive livestock production. This presumably reflects the fact that many farms with extensive rough grazing require few or no changes to meet the certification criteria, and that the rewards in terms of higher livestock prices are significant where conversion costs are low.

Inevitably with such a rate of growth in area, the number of registered organic producers is also rising rapidly. The number rose from 828 to 1568 between April 1997 and 1999 (SA, 1999, p.7).

According to the SA (1999) the farm-gate value of UK organic produce in 1998/9 had reached £50 million at which time the retail market had an estimated value of £390 million. The allocation of this between the major product categories is shown in Table 5.2. Of the combinable crops, wheat accounted for £3.5m with oats the next largest crop worth an estimated £1million.

Table 5.2. Farm-gate value of UK organic production, 1998/9 (Soil Association, 1999)

Product	Tonnes	Value (£m)
Combinable crops	33,500	6.05
Potatoes	17,500	5.25
Cabbages	6,000	2.00
Other vegetables	9,650	5.30
Protected crops and salads	11,000	5.60
Fruit	2,951	2.07
Beef and lamb	no data	3.90
Poultry and pork	no data	3.00
Mushrooms	1,600	3.70
Other *	no data	13.13
Total		50.00

* Value of "other" calculated by accepting total estimate of £50 million

5.3. Economics of organic versus other farming systems

5.3.1. Methodological issues

Most of the attention in this section will concern comparisons of the economics of organic to conventional farming. However, conventional farmers are free to select any methods that suit their system, including elements of organic systems. They can adopt mixed husbandry which utilises animal and green manures, while still electing to apply chemicals which are not permitted to organic farmers. Thus "conventional" farming is not a well-defined system, but is a mixture of that complex of methods which has evolved over time.

For example, there are also a number of "Integrated Farming Systems" (IFS), which share many objectives and some methods with organic farming, but which nevertheless do not qualify as such. A recent paper by Bailey *et al* (2000) undertakes an economic assessment based on four sets of experiments comparing IFS systems to conventional ones. The IFS systems employed disease resistant cultivars, did not invert the soil, sowed cereals a month later than conventional crops, based nutrition on soil and plant chemistry, adopted pest control based on disease thresholds and infestation forecasting, and employed mechanical weeding and low dose herbicides. Thus these systems reduced inorganic fertiliser, herbicide and pesticide use without adopting the tighter restrictions for organic certification. The economic analysis used standardised crop and input prices, and the outcome was that there were no statistically significant differences in the gross margins of the IFS and conventional systems averaged over several years. The possible conclusions from this are that, adopting IFS principles may provide a means for conventional arable farmers to address environmental concerns, without necessarily reducing profit.

Comparing the economics of organic to other types of farming system has raised questions about the appropriate methodological basis to adopt. It is more relevant to use data for commercially operated organic units than to employ economic data from experimental trials. It is also desirable to undertake any comparison between organic and conventional systems over a period of years to allow for variability in yields and market conditions. For some purposes it is also useful to compare the performance of organic farms from the date they begin conversion to a stage of post-conversion maturity, say for eight or more years. However, because of changing market conditions and subsidy payments, the relative success or failure of organic farming over any recent period may not be a reliable pointer to the likely outcome for those beginning conversion now.

A key issue in the comparison is, which conventional farms to select to compare to the organic ones, something which has been compounded by the small number of organic farms on which financial data could be collected when studies commenced a few years ago. For specialist dairy farms, and for cattle and sheep farms selection of comparators is relatively easy, but for arable and mixed farms it is more difficult. While there are many stockless conventional arable farms, there are hardly any stockless arable organic farms which have been available for study. Most organic arable farms have some livestock to generate manure to help balance the nutrient cycle. At this stage there are experimental small scale results on stockless organic farms (Cormack, 1999; Leake 1999) but little in the way of results for commercial farms of this type. Instead in the comparative performance of arable organic farms discussed below, the conventional farms are cereal and general cropping farms with a small proportion of livestock output plus a number of mixed farms on which livestock output typically exceeds that of crops.

Another decision concerns whether to make comparisons on an enterprise gross or net margin basis or on a whole farm basis using Net Farm Income (NFI) or some other aggregate measure of performance. There are strong grounds for adopting the whole farm approach because organic systems require an integration of enterprises; in organic farming systems integration is needed to generate more self-sufficient systems where green or animal manures are produced on the farm, and in livestock systems so that the feed is organic. Also the central role of crop rotation in organic arable farming leads to a greater crop diversity than in conventional farming.

A MAFF financed study at the Welsh Institute of Rural Studies (WIRS) started a number of years ago by drawing together much of the available data on commercial organic farms. This has been supplied to it by institutions such as ADAS Terrington (cropping and mixed) and ADAS Redesdale (cattle and sheep) which have collected the data as part of their own studies of organic farming. By pulling together data in this way WIRS has established small but viable sample numbers of organic farms in a number of categories which can be compared over a number of years to closely matched conventional farms.

The procedure adopted was as follows: "For each organic farm recorded, the aim was to generate a cluster of between 10 and 12 similar conventional farms from the Farm Business Survey (FBS) database ..." for the relevant year clusters (Fowler *et al*, (1998) p.6). Thus, for example, for 1995/96 the performance of a sample of 6 organic cropping farms was compared to that of 73 conventional farms in 6 clusters. "Farms of the same EU type and in the same Farm Business Survey province ..... were initially selected, and then a hierarchical clustering approach was used to pick out farms with similar key characteristics selected to reflect the resource endowment of the holdings." It can be seen in Table 5.3 below that for cropping farms this has resulted in organic and conventional samples with similar output composition and business size.

The distinction between organic and conventional holdings in these comparisons was not an absolutely exclusive one. As Fowler *et al* (1998, p.45) record, for the 1995/96 study "all the results presented for organic farms will have a certified organic land area of greater than 50% by the third year of the study". This qualification mainly affects cropping farms, and it can be noted that in Table 5.3 below only 63% of the land in the average organic farm was either fully organic or in-conversion in 1995/96. For organic dairy farms (Table 5.5) 100% of the land was organic or in conversion, while for the lowland cattle and sheep sample reported more briefly below it was 90%. Some organic farms with non-organic areas may actually manage their land according to organic principles even if land is not registered as in conversion. Also, since the FBS does not differentiate between organic and conventional farms in their survey, some so-called conventional farms may also be managed organically but not certified.

All of the above factors tend to lead to some underestimation of the difference between the two sets of systems in the WIRS study. Nevertheless it is the most comprehensive and up-to-date analysis there is. Moreover its results are not at variance with the small scale studies of cropping systems by Cormack (1999) and Leake (1999). Therefore, in what follows primary reliance will be placed in the results of the WIRS study, which involves annual updating of the comparisons and therefore compares systems over several years.

5.3.2. Some characteristic differences between organic and non-organic farms

In general, crop yields on organic farms are lower than those under conventional farming where inorganic fertilizers and a wide range of pesticides and fungicides are permitted, but, of course, conventional farms incur the high variable cost of these chemicals. For the UK the evidence is that organic cereal yields average around 60% of those for conventional crops (Murphy, 1992; Offermann and Nieberg, 2000, p.27). According to the same sources, organic potatoes appear to average round 50% of conventional crop yields, while other organic vegetables typically achieve yields more comparable to conventional crops. Weed management evidently poses one of the greatest management challenges for the organic arable producer, and weed competition is a major factor (along with nitrogen availability (see Greenland, this volume)) contributing to these lower yields.

The lower yields for organic crops are offset by a combination of substantially higher prices and by various cost savings available in organic systems, so that comparative yields cannot be looked at independently when analysing any differences in profitability.

In livestock farming animals of comparable weight are produced in all systems, and in dairying the average organic milk yield per cow is close to that of conventionally managed animals. Because of lower stocking densities in organic livestock farming, however, performance per cow is not the most useful basis for comparison, and it is more insightful to compare systems using either returns per hectare or returns per whole farm.

It was noteworthy that many of the first farms to move wholly into organic farming were relatively small in area. This was revealed in Murphy's (1992) study of organic farms in 1989/90. At that time his small sample of wholly organic cropping farms averaged only 52.2 hectares as against 150 ha. for conventional cropping farms and 198 ha. for partly organic cropping farms. The same pattern applied to dairy farms, except that the partially organic dairy enterprises had nearly twice the area of the conventional ones. It is not now true that organic farms are typically small in area. As organic farming has moved more into the mainstream established producers have converted to organic production, and many of these had large conventional farming operations. For most of these commercial operators conversion is at least as much about profit as it is about ecological sustainability.

The differences between wholly and partly organic farms is an important one, because the available data (reviewed below) does not relate to wholly organic farms, but includes partly organic farms. In cropping it appears that there are advantages to retaining some conventionally treated areas and having only part of the farm organic. Where there are livestock, in farms of the dairy, mixed, or cattle and sheep types, the tendency is to become wholly organic.

5.3.3. Relative economic performance of organic and non-organic farms

The results in this section are taken from the Welsh Institute of Rural Studies (WIRS) project. There is a published study (Fowler *et al*, 1998) from which the more detailed comparative costings for 1995/96, as presented in Tables 5.3 and 5.5, are taken, and two unpublished sources at the time of writing which elaborate further results (Fowler *et al*, 2000; Fowler 2000). In addition Susan Fowler has kindly provided, by personal communication, the most up-to date results covering 1995/96 to 1997/98, and these have been used for the summary information in Tables 5.4, 5.6 and 5.7.

5.3.3.1. Cropping farms

No organic farms fall into the "largely cereal" category because of the rotational requirements which dictate a mixture of crops including green manures. Thus the nearest category of non-organic farms with which organic cropping farms can be compared is "general cropping" farms. An abbreviated form of the WIRS results for 1995/96 are presented in Table 5.3. It should be remembered that this was a year of especially high prices following the sharp depreciation of sterling after September 1994. All classes of UK farms benefited from this, but prices have subsequently fallen sharply, especially for non-organic products, as the UK pound has steadily appreciated to very high value against the euro currencies.

1995/96 was also the last year of three in which Arable Area Compensation payments were phased in as compensation for reductions in CAP support prices. With the accompanying set-aside payments, this explains the substantial output figures for crop subsidies in Table 5.3.

Two measures of income are shown in Table 5.3 comparing organic to conventional cropping farms. Economists prefer to use Net Farm Income (NFI) because it enables comparison of tenanted and owner-occupied farms as if both types were tenanted. However Occupiers Net Income (ONI) reflects more clearly the profit of individual farm businesses. On both these bases, it can be seen that organic cropping farms on average outperformed conventional

Table 5.3 Comparison of organic and conventional cropping farms, 1995/96 (Fowler *et al*, 1998)

		Organic		Conventional	
No. of farms		6		73, in 6 clusters	
Av. percentage of area organic or in conversion.		63		0	
Av. utilisable agric. area		356.5		266.6	
Outputs		£/farm	£/ha.	£/farm	£/ha.
Main crops	output	233,934	656	191,941	720
	subsidies	57,005	160	55,136	207
Cattle and sheep	output	19,977	56	19,406	73
	subsidies	6,451	18	5,401	20
Other outputs and subsidies		52,727	148	27,254	102
Total output		370,094	1,038	299,138	1,122
Inputs					
Purchased concentrates		2,335	7	9,699	36
Seeds (bought and grown)		22,089	62	13,584	51
Fertilisers		12,134	34	18,839	71
Crop Protection		13,622	38	23,317	87
Labour		47,755	134	45,932	172
Machinery		54,089	152	43,081	162
Other inputs		99,869	280	81,667	306
Total inputs		251,893	707	236,119	886
Net Farm Income (NFI)		125,028	350	70,911	266
Occupiers Net Income (ONI)		138,400	388	92,329	346
Return on tenants capital		49%		27%	

ones in 1995/96. The NFI per hectare of organic farms was substantially higher. A major contribution to this was the higher valuation of stock-in-hand. When this is adjusted for, and other adjustments are allowed for in the calculation of ONI, the average superiority of organic cropping farms on a per hectare basis was still maintained by a margin of 12% (£388 to £346).

Table 5.3 highlights several characteristic differences between the two samples. The six organic farms were 34% larger in Utilisable Agricultural Area, with 63% of their area organic. This underlines that these were not wholly organic units in 1995/96, although most of them became so by 1999/2000. In terms of the composition of output there were no major differences between the two types, although the conventional farms exhibited greater output per hectare in both their livestock and crop enterprises.

On the input side, however, significant differences existed. Purchased concentrate and fertiliser costs per hectare were considerably higher on conventional farms, as expected. All other cost categories shown were also higher on conventional farms, with the exception of seeds, which were more costly on organic farms. As a consequence input costs per hectare on organic farms were 20% less than on conventional farms. This more than cancelled the 8.3% advantage of conventional farms in output per hectare. Also because of their greater size, the total farm measures of profitability for the organic farms were appreciably higher than for the conventional sample.

On the basis of the two indicators in Table 5.4, organic cropping farms have extended their advantage over conventional ones since 1995/6. By 1997/98 their NFI and ONI per hectare were appreciably larger. This mainly resulted from the fact that prices for conventional products have fallen more than those for organic products, reflecting the undersupply of the latter from domestic sources.

Table 5.4 Comparative cropping farms performance 1995/96 - 1997/98 (Fowler, private communication from WIRS)

		1995/96 (£/ha)	1996/97; (£/ha)	1997/98 (£/ha)
Net Farm Income	*Organic*	350	219	142
	Conventional	264	210	40
Occupiers Net Income	*Organic*	388	254	171
	Conventional	347	293	117

5.3.3.2. Dairying

The land areas of the organic and conventional dairy farms compared in Table 5.5 are similar. The conventional farms had a higher stocking rate in terms of both dairy cows and Grazing Livestock Units (GLUs). The larger number of other cattle and breeding sheep on conventional farms contributed to their having an 18% higher average output per hectare. This was achieved despite the fact that they were incurring costs to acquire additional milk quota, whereas the organic farms obtained additional revenue by leasing out or selling unused quota.

The principal differences on the cost side were the much higher labour costs (both paid and imputed) incurred by conventional farms, the much higher fertiliser and purchased concentrate costs, and the higher machinery costs. The

Table 5.5 Comparison of organic and conventional dairy farms 1995/96 (Fowler *et al*, 1998)

		Organic		Conventional	
No. of farms		6		62, in 6 clusters	
Av. area organic or in conversion. (%)		100		n.a.	
Av. utilisable agric. area		97.9		95.2	
Outputs		**£/farm**	**£/ha.**	**£/farm**	**£/ha.**
Dairy	output	139,230	1,422	148,087	1,556
	net quota	4,413	45	-3,848	-40
Other outputs and subsidies		39,470	403	65,322	686
Total output		183,113	1,870	209,561	2,202
Inputs					
Purchased concentrates		14,961	153	35,006	368
Homegrown concentrates		8,366	85	2,013	21
Fertilisers		1,163	12	10,425	110
Labour	Unpaid/family	13,416	137	16,592	174
	Paid	14,170	148	20,638	217
Machinery		25,038	256	30,373	319
Other inputs		63,774	651	57,533	604
Total inputs		140,888	1,439	172,580	1,814
Net Farm Income (NFI)		52,908	540	51,589	542
Occupiers Net Income (ONI)		46,258	472	52,411	551
Return on tenants capital		35%		19%	
Dairy cows/farm		93.9		118.2	
GLUs/farm		139.5		185.8	

only major category of higher costs recorded for the organic farms was for homegrown concentrates. However, as these are outputs of the farm, they are recorded as both outputs and inputs and hence this cost cancels out.

For 1995/96, when the benefits and costs were balanced out, the NFI per hectare was almost the same on both sets of farms. However, the imputed rental cost for the conventional farms was higher (since they owned a higher proportion of their land), and, when this is added back as funds available to farms, the ONI per hectare of conventional dairy farms averaged 17% more than for the organic farms.

Prices for non-organic milk have declined sharply since 1995/96 while the

Table 5.6 Comparative dairy farm performance 1995/96 - 1997/98 (Fowler, private communication from WIRS)

		1995/96 (£/ha)	1996/97 (£/ha)	1997/98 (£/ha)
Net Farm Income	*Organic*	587	477	641
	Conventional	417	398	156
Occupiers Net Income	*Organic*	592	497	614
	Conventional	552	517	346

organic milk market has been buoyant. The dramatic effects of this are clear in Table 5.6, which shows that the income per hectare on organic farms increased up to 1997/98 while on conventional farms there was a very large fall, a situation which has intensified since then. In 2000 the producer price for organic milk was nearly twice the average UK milk price. Organic dairy farming is now on average considerably more profitable than conventional systems, and not surprisingly the interest of dairy farms in conversion has risen appreciably.

5.3.3.3. Lowland cattle and sheep
Cattle and sheep farming is the one area in which organic farms are estimated to perform less well on average than conventional (non-organic) ones. Table 5.7 summarises the per hectare performance of lowland cattle and sheep farms using the data from the WIRS. It can be seen that the organic livestock farms performed markedly worse than conventional ones. The sampled organic farms have slightly larger farm areas and greater total output than the conventional ones, so that their inferior performance is not due to relative lack of economies of size. They also have substantially more of their output from the dairy enterprise, which, given the results of organic dairy farms (above), might have been expected to work strongly in their favour. They incurred noticeably higher costs for paid labour and lower ones for (imputed) family labour than conventional farms, suggesting that a major difference in management structure of the organic farms was responsible for their relatively poor performance.

Because the livestock market is so fragmented, it is the case that certain top quality non-organic cattle (such as Scotch Angus beef) and sheep may be able to obtain prices comparable to those for organic animals, so that there may on average not be such a marked premium for this category of organic farms.

Table 5.7 Comparative lowland cattle and sheep farm performance 1995/96 - 1997/98 (Fowler, private communication from WIRS)

		1995/96 (£/ha)	1996/97 (£/ha)	1997/98 (£/ha)
Net Farm Income	*Organic*	22	-14	-49
	Conventional	149	152	70
Occupiers Net Income	*Organic*	87	27	14
	Conventional	171	174	120

5.3.3.4. Variability in comparative performance

The preceding comparisons have all been presented in terms of averages, and it is important not to ignore the substantial variances in performance in both the organic and conventional samples. This point is powerfully illustrated by Fowler *et al*, (2000), using the same data source as in Tables 5.3 to 5.7 above for the year 1996/97. In that year, on average per hectare, the organic cropping and dairy farms performed much the same as the conventional ones (Tables 5.4 and 5.6), but half the organic samples performed worse than their matched cluster of conventional farms and half better. This underlines the fact that there are successful organic farms and unsuccessful ones, just as is the case in conventional (non-organic) farming. Good management can succeed with any system. Even in the lowland cattle and sheep category, where on average the organic farm performance was weak, two out of eight farms outperformed their matching cluster. Also on this basis organic mixed farms performed particularly well against the conventional clusters, while on horticultural holdings the honours were fairly even in 1996/97. Average organic farming in all categories studied can be more profitable per hectare than average conventional farming, and at the price levels of 1999/2000 is likely to have been so for the majority of organic farms.

5.4. Other issues

5.4.1. Economics of conversion

The process of conversion from conventional to organic farming can be a complex process lasting several years, and it typically involves a loss of income. Lampkin and Measures (1999, p.30,31) identify various possible sources of cost including:

- Output reductions due to changes in husbandry;
- New investments;
- Information and experience gathering;
- Fixed cost increases, typically for labour, depreciation of new machinery, and certification;
- Lack of access to premium prices despite lower yields.

Because there are environmental benefits from organic farming, subsidies are offered to aid conversion. The length of time for conversion is variable, and is typically between two and five years. For that reason conversion aid is offered over a five year period, with higher aid rates in the early years. The next section will briefly review the UK position on subsidies, but this section will confine itself to what is known about conversion costs, since these provide the basis for determining what compensation might be appropriate during conversion.

The UK evidence on conversion costs is actually fairly limited. In early estimates Lampkin and Padel (1994) presented figures based on modelling exercises and case studies comparing two organic dairy farms and two arable farms to conventional farms.

The conclusions (Lampkin and Padel, 1994, p.240) were that "Conversion costs over a five-year period were likely to be of the order of:

- £150 and £200/ha/year for specialist cereal and mainly arable farms, respectively;
- £100/ha/year for specialist dairy farms, but possibly much lower depending on the level of intensity;
- £50 to £100/ha/year for other livestock and mixed livestock/arable farms;
- less than £50/ha/year for hill and upland holdings."

A more recent analysis of conversion costs on specialist dairy and mixed dairy/arable farms has been presented by Haggar and Padel (1996). In some ways this study underlines the difficulties researchers have had in providing reliable measure of the relative economic performance of organic farms. When the three-year study was initiated only 55 possible sample farms in the UK were identified. On initial contact 24 of these were found to be no longer considering conversion and on 14 others conversion was too advanced. In the end the study was left with 10 converting commercial farms to study plus one research farm. These displayed a wide variance of performance during the conversion period, as might be expected in a small sample of rather mixed farms, and with such variation, conclusions about the conversion costs must be treated with caution (as is clearly acknowledged by the report). Nevertheless the conclusions (*ibid*. p.9) were: "On average, the farms incurred costs of conversion .... of approximately £50 per hectare in the first three years of conversion. Higher costs of up to £185 per ha. per year occurred on mixed dairy and arable farms and on rapidly converting specialist dairy farms, whereas those specialist dairy farms that converted in stages had no conversion costs and gained financially up to £180 per ha. per year."

The estimate by Haggar and Padel (1966) of £50/ha/year conversion cost on dairy farms is accepted by Lampkin and Measures (1999, p.31) as being appropriate, and as being significantly lower than earlier estimates which were in the order of £100-200/ha/year. However, the £185/ha/year conversion cost on the mixed dairy and arable farms does perhaps suggest that many arable farms have higher conversion costs, or it may reflect the greater difficulties of adjusting farms with multiple enterprises to organic farming. Even if neither of these conjectures is correct, it does not appear that there is much statistically reliable data available on conversion costs.

5.4.2. Subsidies for organic farming

As part of the 1992 reforms of the CAP, EC Regulation 2078/92 required all member states to introduce schemes to support the conversion of land to organic farming. Around half the EU countries had introduced subsidy schemes in the few years before this, but the UK (in 1994) and countries such as the Netherlands, Portugal, Spain and Ireland then introduced schemes, all of which differ in detail.

The initial UK Organic Aid Scheme (OAS), which ran from 1994 to 1998, had the payment levels shown in Table 5.8 (overleaf).

The scheme provided subsidies on an annually decreasing basis for a five-year conversion period. The standard rate subsidy, averaging £50/ha/year, was lower than the estimates of conversion assumed when the scheme was initiated (the

Table 5.8 UK payments under the Organic Aid Scheme, 1994-1998 (Lampkin and Measures, 1999)

	Year 1 (£/ha.)	Year 2 (£/ha.)	Year 3 (£/ha.)	Year 4 (£/ha.)	Year 5 (£/ha.)	Total (£/ha.)
Standard rate	70	70	50	35	25	250
Less Favoured Areas (England and Wales)	14	14	10	7	5	50
Unimproved Rough Grazing (Scotland and N.I.)	10	10	7	5	5	37

£100 to £200 figures quoted above), although it is in line with Haggar and Padel's (1996) estimated average conversion cost for dairy farms. Also the first scheme made no allowances for the different adjustment costs of different types of lowland farming. The only differentiation from the standard rate was the reduced rates for upland grazing systems. There was an additional £30/year for the first five hectares of any qualifying application, and payments in total were limited to 300 hectares.

The scheme was revised and renamed in 1999. In addition to substantially increasing the rate of aid, it made an important change towards recognising the different adjustment costs of arable systems. This is shown in Table 5.9 by the differentiation of payments according to whether land is eligible for Arable Area Payments (AAPS) or is under permanent crops (fruits, berries and vines), with lower rates for non-eligible improved land and unimproved land.

There is an additional payment per organic unit of £300 in the first year, £200 in the second year and £100 in the third year. These payments recognise additional costs arising from, for example, training and organic certification.

In view of the evidence about conversion costs provided above, the increase in payment rate in the revised OFS can be interpreted as signifying a more positive commitment by the UK towards organic farming. That said it must be accepted that the sums spent to support organic farming have been very small in relation to the total budgetary costs of implementing the Common Agricultural Policy in the UK. The demand for conversion aid overwhelmed the new scheme in 1999, so that, despite the injection of some £9 million additional to the planned amount over the first two budget years, no new applicants could be accepted

Table 5.9 Payments under UK Organic Farming Scheme, 1999 (Lampkin and Measures, 1999)

	Year 1 (£/ha.)	Year 2 (£/ha.)	Year 3 (£/ha.)	Year 4 (£/ha.)	Year 5 (£/ha.)	Total (£/ha.)
Eligible for AAPS or under permanent crops	225	135	50	20	20	450
Improved land not eligible for AAPS	175	105	40	15	15	350
Unimproved land	25	10	5	5	5	50

after November 1999. Spending in England is, however, set to increase substantially, to an expected £137 million, in the seven years covered by The England Rural Development Plan 2000-2006, and new applications for conversion aid will be accepted from 1st April 2001.

One particularly notable aspect of UK policy regarding support for organic farming is that the UK is one of only two EU countries that does not provide post-conversion subsidies for organic production. This is a controversial issue, as demands for post-conversion aid are strongly urged by supporters of organic farming (e.g. Lampkin and Midmore, 2000). At the commercial level there is the argument that UK organic producers are at a competitive disadvantage to other EU producers, and because they do not receive comparable subsidies.

A more important question is whether, since organic production delivers non-market environmental benefits, society should pay subsidies for the on-going production of these in precisely the way that it does for non-market benefits generated in Environmentally Sensitive Area Schemes and Countryside Stewardship. Extensive livestock production in Less-Favoured Areas is subsidised to produce environmental and social benefits. Thus there is no reason in principle why organic farming should not be subsidised for any additional environmental benefits which cannot be captured through the market and are in addition to categories of output for which organic farms are already entitled to subsidy. However, the higher prices achieved for organic produce can be interpreted as reflecting, at least in part, intentional payments by consumers for the additional environmental outputs produced. Thus the question of how much post-conversion subsidy for organic farming would be appropriate is a very difficult one.

5.4.3. Organic premium prices

The need to allocate some land in organic arable farming systems to green manure crops, and the lower yields of organic crops, means that higher prices are needed for organic crops and livestock products (to compensate for the higher price of organic feed) if such systems are to compete with conventional farming systems in terms of profit per hectare. A key question, therefore, for those considering the future of the organic sector in the UK, and for any farmers still considering conversion, is what will happen to the difference between organic and conventional product prices received by producers over the coming years? It is very risky to venture anything resembling forecasts of this, as there is a high margin of uncertainty, and the position will differ from product to product, as well as depending on the marketing channel used. Nevertheless, there do appear to be some encouraging pointers for at least the next few years.

Demand for organic produce in the UK is rapidly outstripping domestic supply, import penetration is increasing, and the market conditions for basic, non-organic produce have fared poorly over the last few years. Taking milk as an example, the average UK producer price has fallen from 25 pence per litre in 1996 to below 17 pence in 2000, while the organic milk price has held firm at 30 pence and above. As Table 5.6 above reveals, this had a dramatic effect after 1995/6 in boosting the relative profitability of organic to conventional milk production, which has prompted an upsurge in dairy farmers interested in converting. Moreover, the high price of organic milk appears to be safeguarded for a number of years by the availability of three-year rolling contracts which guarantee a price of 30 plus pence to 2003. With organic dairy produce imports running at 40% of the market there is no reason to suppose that the organic milk premium will be greatly reduced in the next few years.

The position for organic crops also looks promising for a few years into the future. The delivered price of organic feed wheat imported from other EU countries is currently around three times the price of non-organic feed wheat at £180 to £200 per tonne; this more than compensates for any yield and cost difference in production, and the gap has increased since 1998, so that the figures in Table 5.4 possibly understate the advantage currently enjoyed by organic cropping farms. The current UK price is equivalent to the price at which organic feed wheat could be imported from outside the EU. Even, if as seems likely, the next WTO Round leads to reductions in the import price after 2003, it seems probable that EU organic cereal prices will remain high for several years.

For vegetables, the largest organic sector, the evidence again is that prices substantially above non-organic prices are available. In 2000 early organic potatoes were able to attract £400 per tonne, whereas non-organic earlies brought around £120. For carrots and lettuces a similar picture prevails. Vegetable prices typically vary substantially from year-to-year, and it is quite possible to envisage that there will be high yield years when the organic premia are less than those in 2000 due to oversupply. Moreover, not all the output of organic vegetable producers is of a quality necessary to command the full organic price. However, it would be rash to predict that the producer premium price for organic vegetables, averaged over the next few years, will be any less than the average of the last few years.

The recent announcements by the Iceland supermarket chain about offering frozen organic produce at prices comparable to non-organic produce, and statements from some other supermarkets, have been interpreted as indicating that the producer price gap between organic and non-organic produce will narrow. However, this may not lead to an early erosion of the gap at the producer level. As retail organic sales volumes rise, the costs of distribution and retailing should fall, enabling supermarket retailers to reduce their prices without necessarily passing those reductions through fully to producers. Although supermarkets hold around two-thirds of organic sales, there are other outlets, and these other outlets typically provide higher prices to producers than do supermarkets. Producer groups will undoubtedly continue to work hard to develop these other outlets in order to capture as much of the added-value in distribution as possible, and to mitigate price pressures from the supermarkets. Also the fact remains that the UK is far from self-sufficient in organic produce, and that despite evidence of some reduction in other EU countries in the organic price gap, the costs of importing will help to hold up UK prices. UK retailers will also wish to avoid any uncertainties about the true status of any food they sell as organic, and will want complete confidence in the certification procedures. This may be easier to achieve with home-grown produce than with imports, and some supermarkets have even stepped in to offer farmers grants to expand domestic supply for this reason.

5.5. Conclusion

The evidence is that major categories of organic farming (dairying, cropping, mixed farming and horticulture) are now more profitable per hectare, on average, than non-organic (conventional) farming. As the sector has grown, the average size of organic farming units has increased as existing conventional farms have chosen to convert. Many of the early adopters of organic farming were incomers to the industry, with little farming background, who were dedicated to the environmental principles of organic farming. Growth now is much more heavily based on conversion by established farming businesses attracted by the commercial gains from change. Organic farming, although still small in relation to the UK agricultural sector, is no longer a fringe activity.

It seems reasonable to conclude that the market for UK production of organic milk, cereals, and vegetables certainly looks likely to be strong for quite some years. For those farmers already converted and those now in conversion there is good reason to suppose that on average they will benefit, although as noted above organic farmers do not always outperform "conventional" producers. For those still thinking of conversion, and those who will delay until more money is available for conversion aid, the prospects are less certain, if only because there is greater uncertainty as we look out beyond five years. However there is no obvious reason to suppose that consumer demand for organic food will stop growing or will move into reverse. Competition from quality non-organic food will intensify as farmers increasingly move away from commodity product and become more involved in producing for particular markets and contracts. IFS and other low input systems will grow and try to develop brands in competition with organic farming, and this will tend to erode the organic premium.

Finally it needs to be stated that although conversion to organic farming takes several years and incurs costs, reversion does not incur such costs in general. If the organic price premium declines markedly, organic farmers can readily revert to using inorganic fertiliser and other inputs in excess of organic standards, should that be more profitable.

References

Bailey, A.P., Rehman, T., Park, J., Yates, C.M. and Tranter, R.B. (2000) *Integrated Arable Farming systems – The Future Sustainable Farming System?* Paper presented at the Agricultural Economics Society Conference, University of Manchester, April 2000.

Cormack, W.F. (1999) *Testing a stockless arable organic rotation on fertile soil,* ADAS Terrington, Norfolk.

Fowler, S,. Lampkin, N. and Midmore, P. (1998) *Organic Farm Incomes in England and Wales 1995/96,* Welsh Institute of Rural Studies, Aberystwyth, University of Wales.

Fowler, S., Padel, S., Lampkin, N., Midmore, P. and McCalman, H. (2000) *Factors Affecting the Profitability of Organic Farming in the UK,* Paper presented at the Agricultural Economic Society's Annual Conference, University of Manchester, April 2000.

Fowler, S. (2000) *Economics of organic beef and sheep production,* Welsh Institute of Rural Studies, University of Wales, Aberystwyth.

Haggar, R., and Padel, S. (1996) *Conversion to Organic Milk Production,* Institute of Grassland and Environmental Research, University of Wales Aberystwyth.

Lampkin, N.H., and Padel, S. (1994) *The Economics of Organic Farming: An International Perspective,* CAB International, Wallingford.

Lampkin, N., and Measures, M. (1999) *1999 Organic Farm Management Handbook,* University of Wales, Aberystwyth and Elm Farm Research Centre.

Lampkin, N., and Midmore, P. (2000) *Changing Fortunes for Organic Farming in Europe* Paper presented at the Agricultural Economic Society's Annual Conference, University of Manchester, April 2000.

Leake, A.R. (1999) A report of the results of CWS Agriculture's organic farming experiments 1989-1996, *Journal of the RASE,* **160,** 73-81.

MacKerron D. K. L., Duncan J.M., Hillman J.R., Mackay G.R., Robinson D.J., Trudgill D.L and Wheatley R.J. (1999) Organic farming: science and belief. *Annual Report Scottish Crops Research Institute, Dundee,* 60-72.

Michelson, J., Hamm, U., Wynen, E. and Roth, E. (1999) *The European Market for Organic Products: Growth and Development,* Organic Farming in Europe: Economics and Policy Vol. 7, Universitat Hohenheim.

Murphy, M.C. (1992) *Organic Farming as a Business in Great Britain,* Agricultural Economics Unit, University of Cambridge.

Offermann, F. and Nieberg, H. (2000) *Economic Performance of Organic Farming in Europe,* Organic Farming in Europe: Economics and Policy Vol. 5, Universitat Hohenheim.

Soil Association (1999) *The Organic Food and Farming Report 1999,* Soil Association, Bristol.

Chapter Six

Biodiversity and Environment

Dr J J D Greenwood BA, PhD, CBiol, MIBiol, MIEEM

6.1. Introduction

There are few countries in which a higher proportion of the land is farmed than in Britain. If we do not conserve wild plants and animals on farms, the wildlife of the whole country will be diminished.

Biodiversity has various components:
1. The genetic diversity between individuals within a species. Organic farming, because it needs to adapt to local circumstances rather than override them, may use more crop varieties and breeds.
2. The species richness of the ecological community in a locality. Species richness and the total abundance of individual plants and animals tend to be correlated, though unusually productive ecosystems tend to be dominated by large numbers of individuals of just a few species.
3. Differences between habitats in species composition. This is not markedly affected by differences between farming systems.
4. Differences between geographical localities in the species occurring in similar habitats. Farming, by spreading species far beyond their original geographical ranges, has had a major impact on global biodiversity; organic farming is unlikely to alter this.

This chapter reviews the recent history of farming and wildlife in Britain, the impacts of organic and other non-conventional farming on landscape and biodiversity, and whether such systems can reverse the dramatic loss of wild biodiversity that has occurred in recent decades (see Greenwood 2000). Species richness and the abundance of individuals are the chief focii. Matters relevant to the environment beyond the limits of the farm, such as the pollution of water by pesticides and its eutrophication by fertilisers (including those of organic origin), the release of some greenhouse gases and some of those linked to acid precipitation, the sequestration of carbon, and the use of fossil fuels, are addressed by Stolze *et al* (2000).

6.2. Changes to farming relevant to wildlife

6.2.1. The general picture

Some wild species flourish on farms and historically have benefited by more land being cultivated and, often, by its productivity being increased. But as farmers have managed to harvest a greater proportion of primary productivity there is less edible material left for wildlife, so even these species have declined, not being replaced by anything else. The peak of intensification in Britain, which applied to pastoral as much as to arable regions, occurred during the 1970s and 1980s. It has been driven by economic circumstances and technological developments, particularly mechanisation, pesticides, inorganic fertilisers and new varieties (Chamberlain *et al*, 2000; Fuller, 2000).

6.2.2. Technological developments

Modern machines are more efficient and allow operations to be more independent of weather, so there is less waste available for wildlife to feed on. More frequent operations destroy birds' nests and cause compact soils.

Though the volumes and concentrations of pesticides used have fallen recently, there have been substantial increases in the area being treated, the number of applications per year, and the range of susceptible target organisms. Pesticides often kill species quite unrelated to the target organisms, reducing their populations. Some species resistant to the pesticides or able to recolonise quickly after they have been applied have flourished, so the effects may have been more on the composition of the community of wild plants and animals rather than on total abundance. Even animals not directly affected by pesticides may suffer if the species on which they feed are removed (Campbell *et al*, 2000). Pesticides do not just affect wildlife in the crop itself. Attempts to control the invasion of crops by plants from the margins by applying herbicides to the latter commonly result in the hedge bottom being taken over by aggressive annual weeds that then require repeated applications to keep them under control. Even where pesticides are not applied deliberately to marginal vegetation, they may drift into it, killing both plants and invertebrates.

Average application rates of nitrogen on arable land doubled between 1975 and 1985 and by the early 1990's 85% of grassland was receiving inorganic nitrogen, sometimes injected into the soil, so increasing its effective concentration. The impact on botanical diversity in arable land has been similar to that of herbicides; on grassland it has been far greater. Arable crops that have been bred to utilise high nitrogen supplies produce dense canopies that overwhelm weeds, and fertilisers rapidly reduce the diversity of plants in semi-natural, species-rich grassland. The effects extend to field margins if fertiliser is carelessly scattered over them. Although the greater primary productivity resulting from fertilisers may increase the total numbers of invertebrates in both grassland and arable fields, it tends to reduce their diversity

Conventional farmers use less organic manure than formerly. FYM promotes heterogeneity in the vegetation, because of uneven application, creating gaps in the sward and patches of higher nutrient content. It also increases the soil organic matter and the water–holding capacity of the soil and surface litter, so generally benefits soil-dwelling invertebrates and ground beetles (Carabidae) (see Greenland, this volume). Where cattle waste is applied to land nowadays, it is often in the form of slurry. Its effect on grassland floras is similar to that of inorganic fertilisers and it reduces the numbers of soil-dwelling invertebrates, though it can benefit some flies (Diptera).

6.2.3. Consequences of technology

Modern machinery, inorganic fertilisers and reseeding have caused hay to be largely replaced by silage. This directly reduces floral diversity. They produce a dense uniform sward unsuitable for birds either to feed or nest in. Frequent operations destroy the nests of many birds. The frequent complete removal of vegetation must be detrimental for most above-ground invertebrates.

Improved machinery and the development of pre-emergence herbicides has made autumn-sowing of cereals more effective, so few cereals are now sown in spring. Earlier harvests prevent late-flowering weeds from setting seed; autumn-sown crops restrict establishment of spring-germinating weeds. There are now few overwinter stubbles, formerly important for many farmland birds for winter foraging, as was land left bare after autumn-ploughing and land freshly ploughed in late winter. The denser growth of winter cereals in spring reduces their suitability as nesting sites for field-nesting birds. An effective way of retaining at least some of the wildlife benefits of overwinter stubbles is to adopt regimes of reduced tillage. That is, instead of inversion ploughing, soil and crop residues are cultivated more superficially or, indeed, seed is drilled directly into the residue of the previous crop. The practice is less widely used in Europe than in North America, where its advantages in terms of building soil structure and reducing erosion are particularly important.

Soil fertility was classically maintained, and pests controlled, by the use of rotations, generally involving stock even in mainly arable regions. Pesticides and fertiliser have allowed arable farmers to simplify their rotations and get rid of stock. There has been a steep decline in mixed farming. Bare fallow is much less widely used, as are undersown leys, which boost insect numbers in the crop, provide habitat post-harvest and boost earthworm numbers in arable crops grown subsequently. On mixed farms, mobile species can move around as various crops are harvested and may benefit from having a variety of crops and field types within their home-ranges. This appears to be true for brown hares. Many birds in primarily pastoral landscapes also appear to benefit from having some arable land available.

Machines have allowed the drainage, ploughing and reseeding of almost all formerly unimproved lowland (and much upland) grassland, with intensification boosted further by inorganic fertilisers. Floral diversity has been significantly reduced, as have the numbers of birds breeding on lowland wet meadows. Greatly intensified grazing (especially by sheep in the uplands) has produced short, tight swards that are unsuitable for most foraging birds and probably reduce invertebrate diversity.

Non-crop habitats hold a substantial proportion of the biodiversity on agricultural land. Modern machinery allows the easier destruction of such habitats and a substantial proportion of hedges were removed or fell into dereliction in the second half of the 20th century. Hedges and the associated field margins provide living-space and corridors for the dispersal of many species (O'Connor and Shrubb 1986; Vickery *et al*, 1998). Many plants, including rare arable weeds, find refuge under them, and they provide food and shelter for many animals.

6.2.4. Organic farming is different

Because organic farmers do not use modern pesticides and fertilisers, they tend to maintain mixed farms, balanced rotations and the use of organic manures. Their holistic philosophy stresses the value of biodiversity, so one would expect them to manage non-crop habitats sympathetically. That does not mean they are old-fashioned but that their techniques are different from those of conventional farmers. These differences may benefit wildlife. It is, however, true that some ways of benefiting wildlife are not readily available to organic farmers. For example, since they normally use deep and frequent cultivation to control weeds, it is difficult for them to adopt a reduced tillage regime.

6.3. Recent history of farmland wildlife

6.3.1. Expectations
Given that there have been huge changes in agricultural practices, many of which undoubtedly affect wild plants and animals at the local scale, one would expect there to have been changes in the national populations of many species associated with farmland.

6.3.2. Plants
The flora of Britain changed substantially in the second half of the 20th century. Although some introduced species increased, most of the changes were declines, some of them continuations of earlier losses. As expected, plants of grasslands and arable fields are amongst the biggest losers. The other critical habitats are heathlands, largely lost through conversion to agriculture, and wetlands, drained or widely suffering eutrophication from agricultural run-off.

6.3.3. Invertebrates
Invertebrates recently extinct and threatened in Britain tend to live in habitats which are maintained by certain traditional forms of land management, but their loss cannot generally be blamed on recent agricultural intensification. Unfortunately, there is little information on changes in invertebrates more generally. The available evidence points to widespread declines among many butterflies and some moths (Fox, 2000). The causes include the loss of unimproved grasslands of all sorts, including arable field margins.

   Nationwide data for 1969-88 show that six out of the seven species of cereal aphids studied showed only slight long-term trends in abundance, though the main aphid pest of cereals, *Sitobion avenae*, had doubled its numbers despite the substantial attempts to control it. In contrast, a 20-year monitoring programme by the Game Conservancy Trust on a 62 km^2 area of arable farming indicated that total aphid numbers had declined by about 80% during 1970-89 (Sotherton and Self, 2000). There were either no trends in the abundance of other sorts of insects or they had declined (as had harvestmen and spiders); no groups increased. The declines have probably been driven partly by the use of insecticides (especially summer applications) and partly by the loss of food consequent on the use of herbicides.

6.3.4. Mammals
Known changes in mammal populations, many of them dramatic, have been consequent on habitat loss, persecution or protection, or interactions with introduced species rather than on agricultural practices.

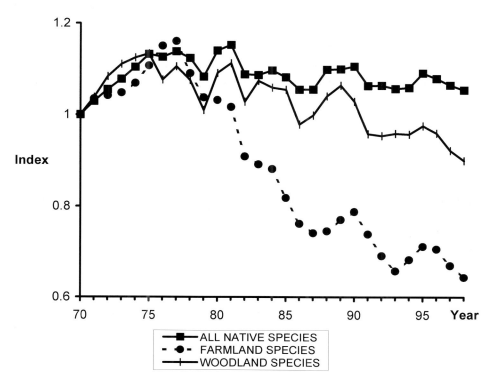

Figure 6.1. Population indices of farmland and woodland birds in Britain. For index, see Gregory *et al* (1999).
(Reproduced with the permission of BTO, DETR and RSPB)

6.3.5. Birds

Because of a long-standing network of volunteer fieldworkers, birds are well monitored and have proved valuable indicators of the fortunes of wildlife. Though many species are doing well, many woodland birds and the majority of farmland species are declining (Figure 6.1.). While approximately equal numbers of species of woodland birds have declined in numbers as have increased during the last 30-40 years, the losses of farmland birds have far outweighed the gains. The declining species are associated with a variety of habitats within farmland and have various diets; it is their use of farmland that is the common thread. Furthermore, it is the farmland specialists that have declined, rather than more generalist species that happen to use farmland. The steep decline began in the mid-1970s, lagging just a few years behind a period of rapid intensification of British agriculture (Chamberlain *et al*, 2000).

The losses have not been confined to the arable landscapes of eastern Britain, commonly regarded as those where agricultural intensification and change have been most marked. Rates of population decline have been as great in pastoral as in arable landscapes and local extinctions of farmland bird species have indeed been more common in pastoral landscapes. For example, the Lapwing *Vanellus vanellus*, which uses pastures, especially damp pastures, to a great extent, declined by almost 50% in England and Wales (and probably in much of Scotland and Ireland) during 1987-98, following considerable losses in the preceding three decades.

In the majority of species the declines are associated with decreased survival rather than lower breeding success per breeding attempt, which suggests that changes in the winter environment rather than in the summer may be generally more important (Baillie *et al*, 1997). The exact causes of the declines are different for different species. The most important factors seem to be: the reduction in availability of seeds and invertebrates through the use of herbicides and pesticides, the loss of winter stubbles and the intensification of grazing; the unsuitability of autumn-sown crops and dense rye-grass swards as breeding habitats; the disruption of breeding by the cutting of silage; and the loss of habitat variety.

6.4. Landscape effects of alternative farming systems

Organic farming standards include the sympathetic management of the landscape. Indeed, the efficacy of organic farming depends in part on practices that benefit the landscape, such as maintaining hedges to reduce the spread of wind-born diseases and to provide shelter for predators that may help control pests. Furthermore, organic farmers tend to be fundamentally more sympathetic to maintaining landscape quality than are conventional farmers and more likely to undertake measures aimed at doing so (ENTEC, 1995).

There is much opinion, but little hard evidence, from Britain or elsewhere, as to how these differences translate into differences in landscape. However, it is clear that organic farmers are more likely than conventional to plant new woodlands and hedges and to maintain tall, bushy hedges and hedgerow trees. Their fields tend to be smaller. Organic mixed lowland farms tend to have more pasture and substantially more leys than their conventional counterparts. As expected from their non-use of herbicides, they have more bare plough over winter and are more likely to plant cereals in spring. Unexpectedly, one sample of organic farms in lowland England had no more overwinter stubble than their conventional counterparts, perhaps because the conventional farmers had made so much use of set-aside schemes.

Given the importance of livestock in organic systems, one would expect mixed farming to be commoner in the organic sector. This appears to be the case, although many organic farmers who are unwilling to take on the additional burdens of managing livestock attempt to manage their farms as wholly arable enterprises, using stockless rotations (Lampkin, 1990).

6.5. The effects of organic farming on biodiversity

6.5.1. Approaches to the problems

It is not easy to study the effects of alternative farming systems on animals and plants. One problem is that wildlife may respond only slowly to a change in management. Organic farms are just islands in a sea of conventional farming: not only may animals and plants be slow to colonise such isolated patches of suitable habitat but the patches may be too small to sustain viable populations of some species.

Such problems of scale are particularly acute in studies that are based on small experimental plots. Furthermore, such small-scale studies tend to concentrate on just one or a few components of the management regime (typically, fertilisers and pesticides), so that they do not embrace the holistic approach to organic farming. On the other hand, they do allow clearer identification of the causes of the biodiversity differences between farming systems than do studies that compare actual organic and conventional farms (and which thus embrace the whole suite of differences in management). Even when comparing actual farms, investigators have tended to compare fields with similar crops. This prevents the effects of the farming system from being confounded by differences between crops. But the latter may themselves be a consequence of adopting different farming systems: for example organic farms are more likely to be mixed and to sow cereals in spring. The best approach is undoubtedly to follow the development of the flora and fauna during and after conversion, in comparison with nearby farms that continue with a conventional regime, but there have been almost no such studies.

Another problem is that many of the existing studies are based on just single farms (or pairs of farms), so there is no formal way of determining whether differences in wildlife are, indeed, the result of a difference in the farming system or some other factor. Even well-replicated studies tend to be limited to fairly small geographical areas. Thus the only way to reach general conclusions is to draw together all the studies and weigh up their conclusions. The presentations in this section are based on such an approach. In each subsection, an indication is given of the number and magnitude of the studies providing evidence.

6.5.2. Weeds in arable fields

Organic farmers often control weeds well through rotations, mechanical or hand weeding, cultivation techniques, manipulating soil conditions, and biological control. However, the total control of weeds is rarely necessary and organic farmers may choose to target their efforts at critical periods in the growth of crops; they may choose to use a residual weed population to provide living space for the insects and other organisms that can assist in the control of pests and diseases; they may, indeed, choose to retain some weeds as a contribution to biodiversity conservation, deliberately adopting practices designed to do this, though there is little hard information on these points. Several studies have shown both cereals and rootcrops to be weedier on organic farms. The difference is more marked in the centre of crops than towards their edges, where even in conventional systems weeds may invade from the field margins. The chief difference in overall abundance is in broad-leaved weeds. Indeed, some grasses sometimes flourish more in the conventional crop.

What are weeds to the farmer are wild flowers to many others and particular attention has focussed on rare arable weeds, many of them specialists that flourished in the arable ecosystem for thousands of years until farmers discovered how to control them. A recent study in southern England found that such species tend to be more frequent on organic fields.

6.5.3. Weeds of arable field margins

Field margins contain a substantial proportion of the botanical biodiversity on most farms. Common observation suggests that conventional farming has impoverished this flora but there have been few formal investigations. A small Finnish study showed a slightly greater species diversity in organic margins but a larger English one did not, though it did find differences in species composition and, in particular, more nationally declining species in the organic margins. It may be that many plant species extinguished from field margins under conventional management take a long time to recolonise after conversion to organic.

6.5.4. Grassland plants

Organically managed permanent grassland is frequently richer in plant (and animal) species than conventional. However, the crucial factor for grassland is the intensity of management, especially nitrogent input (organic or inorganic). The flora of organic short-term leys is often no richer than that of conventional leys because under both regimes the ley is established with high-productivity seed mixes and fertilised to enhance its productivity.

6.5.5. Soil animals

A study based on six sites in southern England showed that both earthworms and leatherjackets (Tipulidae larvae) were more abundant under organic than conventional cereals, as were flies (Diptera) particularly associated with manure. But numbers of dipterans generally, of beetles, and of total invertebrates were not significantly different. Most other studies of the effects of organic farming on soil animals (there appear to have been fewer than a dozen in the whole of Europe, all on fairly small scale) have concentrated on earthworms. These tend to be more abundant in organic arable fields than conventional, perhaps because organic farms use more organic manures and rotational leys.

Earthworm numbers on grassland are generally higher than on arable. The few studies that have been done show that they are not systematically greater under organic grassland than conventional. A single study showed more tardigrades, mites and nematodes under organic grassland (in Wales) but another showed ground-beetles (Carabidae) to be more abundant on conventional grassland (in Aberdeenshire).

6.5.6. Invertebrates in arable crops

There have been a number of small-scale studies of invertebrates in arable crops (mostly cereals) from Europe and other temperate regions. Some show more invertebrates in total under organic systems but others show no difference. Occasionally, perhaps because of poor growth of an organic crop, the conventional crop holds more. Differences in soil type seem as important as differences in farming system.

A large-scale study in Denmark showed that most arthropods were substantially more abundant in organic fields (although conventional cereals were infested by more aphids and thrips). In contrast, two major studies in southern England (Moreby *et al*, 1994; Brookes *et al*, 1995) found no overall differences between farming systems in total invertebrate abundance. In one, but not the other, this may have been because samples were only taken in the edges of the crop (where the Danish study showed differences to be less marked). The difference between the Danish and English results probably depends also on differences in the exact management applied. For example, summer aphicides were used in the Danish study areas, but not in the area covered by an English study, and the organic fields in the latter had few weeds. There may also be regional differences, as shown by the results of studies of Collembola (springtails) in winter wheat in three parts of southern England: not only were there big differences between regions in the abundance of individual species, but the differences between organic, integrated and conventional farming systems were not the same in the three regions.

6.5.7. Ground beetles (carabidae) in arable fields

Arable farms hold plenty of carabid beetles and much attention has been focussed on them, perhaps because they are relatively easy to study. From about ten studies, it is clear that organic crops tend to hold more individual species of carabids than do conventional crops but there are big differences between species, with some favouring conventional crops. At one of two study sites in Aberdeenshire, total carabid abundance was greater in conventional potatoes than organic but this was entirely because of one particularly abundant species, *Pterostichus melanarius*, which appeared to be favoured by the microclimate under the denser canopy of the conventional crop. This is an illuminating case because the same species has generally been found to be more abundant in organic crops, perhaps because the more abundant weeds in the organic crops provide it with shelter. Once again, details are important.

Two studies have simultaneously studied the effects of management system and crop type on carabids. In one of them it was found that crop type was substantially more important than organic management in determining numbers.

6.5.8. Spiders in arable fields

Like some carabids, spiders are important predators and are therefore of interest to organic farmers hoping to control pests with the aid of "natural enemies". Organic farming is likely to benefit spiders through providing structurally more complex habitats (through greater weediness or undersowing). The rather few relevant studies of spiders do, indeed, indicate that there are more species and individuals in organic crops but this is by no means universal; some species of spiders may sometimes be more abundant in conventional fields.

6.5.9. Butterflies on mixed farms

On intensively farmed land butterflies are largely restricted to field boundaries. Even these have been degraded as butterfly habitat by intensification. Herbicides have destroyed larval food plants and the perennial species that are important sources of nectar; fertiliser scattered into margins has encouraged aggressively competitive weeds of little value to butterflies; and insecticide drift may have killed them and their caterpillars. It is not therefore surprising that a three-year study of mostly mixed farms in southern England showed the conventional to have fewer butterflies, in terms of both species an individuals, than organic (Feber, *et al* 1997). The difference was particularly marked within the fields, where it appeared to depend on the pattern of succession of crops rather than on crop management practices, but even the boundaries were richer on the organic than on the conventional farms. The less mobile species, which are unable to cope with the frequent sudden changes in the habitat associated with intensive farming, showed the greatest impact of differences in the farming system. Other reasons for the superiority of organic systems for butterflies are the greater variety of crops and of non-crop habitats, the greater number of larval food plants and nectar-bearing flowers, and the bulkier hedges, providing food resources, overwintering sites and shelter during the flying season.

In contrast to the general result, Large and Small Whites *Pieris brassicae* and *P. rapae* were both as common on conventional as on organic farms, perhaps encouraged by the greater quantities of oil-seed rape grown on the former. Both are agricultural pests.

6.5.10. Mammals

There have been few studies of the reaction of mammals to organic practices. More Wood Mice *Apodemus sylvaticus* were found on conventional winter wheat than on organic spring wheat in southwest England, perhaps because of the denser crop cover.

6.5.11. Birds

Bird populations increased on two mixed farms subsequent to conversion from intensive to organic management. It is not clear how far the results depended on the organic prescriptions that were adopted or on other features of the new regimes, such as the protective fencing of hedges, the planting of woods and shelter belts, and the provision of nest boxes.

The British Trust for Ornithology studied birds on 22 organic farms in England and Wales (Chamberlain *et al*, 1999). The sample included arable, mixed and pastoral enterprises, each paired with a nearby conventional farm. Skylark *Alauda arvensis* population densities on organic farms averaged twice those on conventional farms. (An intensive study showed that this was partly because conventional cereals rapidly become too dense for breeding; conventional setaside was as attractive as organic crops). As in a similar Danish study, most other species were commoner on the organic farms. This was especially true in winter, a season when another study showed that seed-eaters appeared particularly to be attracted to organic farms. Differences in hedgerow management account for the attractiveness of organic farms for some of these species but not for all.

6.5.12. The overall impact of organic farming on the abundance and diversity of plants and animals

In general, it appears that non-crop plants and animals are more abundant and diverse on organic than on conventional farms. There are several important caveats to this generalisation: the evidence from grassland, which is meagre, suggests that the benefits of organic practices are less than they are on arable farms; the differences are often highly species-specific and even within species they are not necessarily constant; the differences between the biota of organic and conventional farms may be less than those between different soils and crop-types; and many of them may depend more on the management of non-crop habitats than on strictly organic prescriptions. Most importantly, we may expect that organic farmers are more likely to maintain mixed farming or, at least, more complex rotations. Yet the studies so far made of organic farms have almost invariably involved comparing similar farms or (generally) fields with the same crops, so there is little evidence of the impact of this major difference in management.

6.6. Integrated farming

The aim of integrated farming systems is to use techniques derived from both conventional and organic systems in a way that maximises the benefits derived from each while minimising the disadvantages. Because there is no agreed regime for such systems, the extent to which different practices are adopted varies greatly, effectively covering the full spectrum from conventional to organic. Various experiments, demonstration projects and schemes have been operated in Britain and overseas, the major current ones being LINK-IFS and LEAF (Holland *et al*, 1994a; Burn 2000).

An early review suggested that integrated farming generally enhanced biodiversity (Table 6.1). Indeed, one of the reasons that many farmers are reluctant to adopt the approach is that it tends to result in weedier fields. Since then, results have seemed less clear-cut. Thus, in one study earthworms were eliminated by conventional treatment while in another there were more under the conventional than the integrated system; at LINK-IFS sites, the abundances of ground-beetles (Carabidae) and linyphiid spiders were mainly determined by location, year and crop type, with the farming system having little effect. The general conclusion is that, while the manipulation of the cropping regime and husbandry may be important, significant benefits to biodiversity are only likely if farmers also manage non-crop habitats sympathetically.

6.7. Conclusions. Can organic farming be the saviour of farmland wildlife?

6.7.1. Are organic systems necessarily good for biodiversity?

Organic systems (and, to a lesser extent, integrated systems) tend to produce

Table 6.1. The numbers of studies showing changes in abundance or diversity of various sorts of animals under integrated farming systems, based on a review of seven UK and five other European studies (Holland *et al*, 1994b).

	Increase	No change or variable	Decrease	Not studied
"Beneficial arthropods"	7	2	0	3
Birds and mammals	1	1	0	10
Earthworms	4	1	0	7
Soil microbes	1	2	0	9

greater biodiversity than does conventional farming. The benefits vary, however, according to location, crop type and species, to such an extent that biodiversity is sometimes lower under organic regimes.

Highly intensive farming is bad for wildlife because it is geared to maximising the proportion of the primary productivity that is harvested, which minimises the amount available for wildlife. In principle, an intensive organic farm may have little more space on it for wildlife than an intensive conventional farm. An organic farmer may be as successful in controlling weeds as his conventional neighbour; he may manage short-term leys almost as intensively as the latter does; he may plough up ancient pastures, drain wet meadows, or bring marginal hill land into cultivation. The main benefits to wild flora and fauna do not all emerge automatically from organic farming but from positive steps taken with the express purpose of obtaining such benefits. They may be taken because of personal ethical beliefs, because they are thought to deliver better control of pests, or because the official standards require it. Thus whether wildlife will benefit from a wider uptake of organic farming will depend both on the attitudes of new converts and the standards applied. If conversion is increasingly stimulated by financial support, the attitudes of new converts may be less wildlife-friendly than those of established organic farmers. However, there are moves to strengthen those parts of the standards specifically designed for the benefit of wild plants and animals.

6.7.2. Pesticides

Reducing the direct and indirect effects of pesticides is one of the main benefits of organic farming for biodiversity. Economic pressures and more widely available advice have caused many conventional farmers to reduce their use of pesticides and to use them in less damaging ways. Much greater moves in this direction, focussed on the benefits to wildlife, are possible without farmers adopting fully organic regimes (Ewald and Aebischer, 1999)

6.7.3. How else to benefit wildlife?

There is considerable evidence and practical advice on highly effective ways of enhancing the wildlife value of farmland (O'Connor and Shrubb, 1986; Lack, 1992; Andrews and Rebane, 1994; Vickery *et al*, 1998). It includes the better management of farm woodlands, hedges, field margins, ditches and their banks; the provision of wildlife strips (such as "beetle banks") around or across fields; managing the marginal areas of crops as "conservation headlands", with much-reduced pesticide use; maintaining overwinter stubbles and undersown spring cereals; the management of setaside to yield wildlife benefit; and maintaining heterogeneity of both crop and non-crop habitats. Such practices have been widely used to enhance the populations of game in particular, but wildlife populations generally also benefit. They can be applied to both conventional and organic farms and are likely to succeed in enhancing biodiversity because that is their objective.

The UK Biodiversity Action Plan includes many farmland species and several farm habitats, such as cereal field margins, various types of grassland, and species-rich and ancient hedges. Partly as a result, schemes are operated to encourage some of the above practices; the Environmental Sensitive Areas scheme, focussed on BAP habitats, is directed at enchancing the landscape and wildlife value of discrete areas; the Countryside Stewardship scheme focuses on key landscapes, including grasslands and the management of grassy field margins; the Arable Stewardship scheme supports overwinter stubbles, undersown spring cereals, conservation headlands and field-margin management, and wildlife strips (Swash *et al*, 2000). A scheme to promote mixed farming and the use of traditional rotations could benefit wildlife greatly, on both conventional and arable farms.

6.7.4. A coherent approach

The conservation of biodiversity on farmland is patchy in two senses. First, organic farms (and other "wildlife friendly" farms) are islands in a sea of intensive conventional farmland. This reduces their effectiveness as wildlife habitat. Second, the various schemes promoted by government and other bodies to enhance wildlife on farms do not, despite the Biodiversity Action Plan, comprise an integrated system. This reduces their effectiveness in achieving the overall objective. The problem is exacerbated by environmental objectives not yet having become a core element of agricultural policy. Were there to be that shift, backed by a coherent framework of practical schemes, there could be a recovery from the biodiversity losses of the late 20th century. Organic farming, though not the whole solution, will have its part to play in that process.

References

Andrews, J. and Rebane, M. (1994) *Farming & Wildlife*. RSPB, Sandy.

Baillie, S. R., Gregory, R. D., and Siriwardena, G. M. (1997) Farmland bird declines: patterns, processes and prospects. In: *Biodiversity and Conservation in Agriculture. BCPC Symposium Proceedings 69*. British Crop Protection Council, Farnham, pp 65-87.

Brooks, D., Bater, J., Jones, H., and Shah, P. A. (1995) Invertebrate and weed seed food-sources for birds in organic and conventional farming systems. *BTO Research Report 154, Part IV*. British Trust for Ornithology, Thetford.

Burn, A. J. (2000) Pesticides and their effects on lowland farmland birds. In: *Ecology and Conservation of Lowland Farmland Birds*. (Eds. N.J. Aebischer, A.D. Evans, P.V. Grice, and J. Vickery). British Ornithologists' Union, Tring pp 89-104.

Campbell, L. H., Avery, M. I., Donald, P., Evans, A. D., Green, R. E., and Wilson, J. D. (1997) *A review of the indirect effects of pesticides on birds. JNCC Report. No. 227*. Joint Nature Conservation Committee, Peterborough.

Chamberlain, D. E., Fuller, R. J., Bunce, J. C., Duckworth, J. C., and Shrubb, M. (2000) Changes in the abundance of farmland birds in relation to the timing of agricultural intensification in England and Wales. *Journal of Applied Ecology* **17**.

Chamberlain, D. E., Wilson, J. D., and Fuller, R. J. (1999) A comparison of bird populations on organic and conventional farm systems in southern Britain. *Biological Conservation* **88**, 307-320.

ENTEC. (1995) *Effects of organic farming on the landscape*. A Report to the Countryside Commission.

Ewald, J. A. and Aebischer, N. J. (1999) *Pesticide use, avian food resources and birds densities in Sussex. JNCC Report No. 296*. Joint Nature Conservation Committee, Peterborough

Feber, R. E., Firbank, L., Johnson, P. J., and Macdonald, D. W. (1997) The effects of organic farming on pest and non-pest butterfly abundance. *Agriculture, Ecosystems and Environment* **64**, 133-139.

Fox, R. (2000) Butterflies and moths. In: *The Changing Wildlife in Britain & Ireland*. (Ed. D.L. Hawksworth). Taylor & Francis, London

Fuller, R. J. (2000) Relationships between recent changes in lowland British agriculture and farmland bird populations: an overview. In: *Ecology and Conservation of Lowland Farmland Birds.* (Eds. N.J. Aebischer, A.D. Evans, P.V. Grice and J. Vickery). British Ornithologists' Union, Tring. pp 5-16.

Greenwood, J. J. D. (2000) *The impact of organic farming on biodiversity. BTO Research Report No. 246.* British Trust for Ornithology, Thetford.

Gregory, R. D., Gibbons, G. W., Imprey, A., and Marchant, J. H. (1999) *Generation of the headline indicator of wild bird populations.* B.T.O. Research Report 221. British Trust for Ornithology, Thetford and Royal Society for the Protection of Birds, Sandy.

Holland, J. M., Frampton, G. K., Cilgi, T., and Wratten, S. D. (1994a) Arable acronyms analyses - a review of integrated arable farming systems research in Western Europe. *Annals of Applied Biology* **125**, 399-438.

Holland, J. W., Thomas, S. R., and Courts, S. (1994b) *Phacelia tanacetifolia* flower strips as a component of integrated farming. In: *Field Margins: Integrating Agriculture and Conservation BCPC Monograph 58* (Ed. N. Boatman). British Crop Protection Council, Farnham, pp 215-220.

Lack, P. (1992) *Birds on Lowland Farms.* HMSO, London.

Lampkin, N. H. (1990) *Organic Farming.* Farming Press, Ipswich.

Moreby, S. J., Aebischer, N. J., Southway, S. E., and Sotherton, N. W. (1994) A comparison of the flora and arthropod fauna of organically and conventionally grown winter wheat in southern England. *Annals of Applied Biology* **125**, 13-27.

O'Connor, R. J. and Shrubb, M. (1986) *Farming and Birds.* Cambridge University Press, Cambridge.

Sotherton, N. W. and Self, M. J. (2000) Changes in plant and arthropod biodiversity on lowland farmland: an overview. In: *Ecology and Conservation of Lowland Farmland Birds.* (Eds N.J. Aebischer, A.D. Evans, P.V. Grice and J. Vickery). British Ornithologists' Union, Tring, pp 26-35.

Stolze, M., Piorr, A., Häring, A., and Dabbert, S. (2000*) The Environmental Impacts of Organic Farming in Europe.* (Organic Farming in Europe: Economics and Policy Volume 6). University of Hohenheim, Stuttgart-Hohenheim, Germany.

Swash, A., Grice, P. V., and Smallshire, D. (2000) The contribution of the UK Biodiversity Action Plan and agri-environment schemes to the conservation of farmland birds in England. In: *Ecology and Conservation of Lowland Farmland Birds.* (Eds. N.J. Aebischer, A.D. Evans, P.V. Grice and J. Vickery). British Ornithologists' Union, Tring pp 36-42.

Vickery, J. A., Fuller, R. J., Henderson, I. G., Chamberlain, D. E., Marshall, E. J. P., and Powell, W. (1998) *Use of cereal fields by birds: a review in relation to field margin management. BTO Research Report No 195.* British Trust for Ornithology, Thetford.

Chapter Seven

Food Quality and Health

Professor C M Williams BSc, PhD
Professor T H Pennington MB BS, PhD, DSc(Hon), FRCPath, FRCP(E), FRSE, FMedSci
Dr O Bridges BA, MA, PhD, DipEnvPractice, MInstEnvSci
Professor J W Bridges BSc, PhD, DSc, MRCPath, FIBiol, CBiol, FRSC, CChem MInstEnvSci, FIOSH, FRSA

7.1. Introduction

There can be little doubt that the notion of healthiness is an important factor contributing to the willingness of the public to pay premium prices for organic foods. In the recent House of Lords Report on "Organic farming and the European Union" (1999) the reasons for consumers purchasing organic foods rather than conventional foods were reviewed. A Health Which survey in April 1997 found that 83% of organic food consumers bought it because they wanted to avoid pesticides. A 1997 survey for Sainsbury's also showed that a principal reason for buying organic foods was health/safety. A survey by MORI in June 1999 identified that of those purchasing organic foods, over half did so because they believed it to be safe and healthy.

Claims that food crops grown using chemical fertilisers and pesticides in conventional systems have adverse effects on the health of animals and man have been prevalent since the early 1940s, although the evidence for such claims has been largely anecdotal (Daldy, 1940). The view that conventional methods of growing might be disadvantageous to human health appears to be based on perceptions that this method of food production can:

- Lead to poorer soil quality and nutrient composition leading to lower nutrient contents of crops and animals and thereby inadequate intakes in humans;
- Reduce levels of protective antioxidants, anticancer compounds, etc. in plant foods;
- Cause accumulation of synthetic agrochemical residues in crops and animals resulting in toxicological levels of exposure in humans.

Conversely, it has also been suggested that application of manure and reduced use of fungicides and antibiotics in organic farming could result in a greater contamination by micro-organisms or microbial products of organic foods. Surprisingly these perceptions have received little critical review and the aim of this chapter is to evaluate their validity, based on the available scientific evidence. In comparing effects of organic and conventional growing on food quality, the nutrient levels of food (fats, proteins, carbohydrates, vitamins and minerals), as well as the content of non-nutrients (anutrients) including natural toxins (see section 7.4.) must be taken into account. Assessment of the relative quality of foods produced by the two agricultural methods are only valid if they involve comparisons of identical strains of plants/animals grown and housed under similar conditions, since these genetic and environmental variables may play an important part in the health impacts subsequently observed in animal and human feeding studies. Unfortunately few of the studies reviewed in the present chapter can be considered to fulfil these rigorous criteria.

7.2. Effect of agricultural methods on nutritional quality

The developing popularity of organically grown foods has originated, in part, from an increasingly widespread perception that this production method results in food of higher nutrient quality (particularly protein, vitamins and minerals). However evidence that can clearly support or negate this perception remains equivocal, with the number of systematically controlled studies that have compared organic versus conventionally grown crops disappointingly small. The confusion is well illustrated by two diametrically opposed statements currently published on the web. Whereas the website of the American Council on Science and Health states "Not a single published study has shown any difference in the nutrient content of organic versus conventional farm produce", the Health Journal supports the view that organic food is healthier than conventionally grown food "...based on research in Denmark and Germany showing that organically grown foods contain higher levels of nutrients". Three reviews of the published literature in this area in recent years have failed to draw definitive conclusions (Lampkin, 1990; Woese, 1997; Worthington, 1998), although each indicate trends for higher concentrations of some nutrients in organic compared with conventionally grown produce. Worthington (1998) also considers the evidence for relatively adverse effects of conventional feeds on animal health to be convincing.

The present review will evaluate the evidence for differences in the nutritional quality of conventionally grown versus organic produce based on; nutrient analyses of crops grown under the different conditions, health outcomes in controlled animal feeding studies and a brief consideration of a small number of observational studies in humans.

7.2.1. Comparison of nutrient composition of organic and conventional crops

Woese (1997) considered over 150 comparisons of conventionally and organically produced foods published between 1924 and 1994. The author drew attention to the shortcomings of many of the studies, the limited background information in the papers and the lack of rigorously controlled conditions. Many studies compared produce available in markets where the validity of the 'organic' produce could not be confirmed. The long period of the review (1924-1994) also means that growing conditions for the foods classified as 'conventionally grown' is likely to have varied considerably over time, due to changes in agricultural practice.

The review concentrated on food groups, including cereals, potatoes, vegetables, fruits, wine, beer, bread, cakes, milk, meat, eggs and honey. Most of the studies were conducted in Germany. In some cases a sufficient number of studies were available for comparison, e.g. for cereals there were 30 studies, vegetables 70 and potatoes 22. Fewer studies were available for animal products, with 9 studies on milk and only 4 on meat, all of which were for pork. With respect to the studies on crops, there was clear evidence for higher nitrate concentrations in vegetables grown under conventional conditions, although this did not apply to cereals or potatoes. In the case of cereals (19 studies), the data showed that for wheat (10 studies), lower protein levels were found in samples obtained through organic cultivation systems. This has undesirable consequences for baking quality where a high protein level is needed to ensure optimal loaf volume. All concentrations were expressed in terms of weight of fresh material.

No differences were found in the mineral, trace element or B vitamin levels of organically or conventionally grown cereals, potatoes or vegetables. Also in 27 comparative studies conducted on vegetables, no differences were found in levels of vitamin A or β carotene. However there was moderately strong and consistent evidence for lower levels of vitamin C in conventionally grown potatoes and 50% of the studies conducted on vegetables also showed organic produce to have higher vitamin C levels, with the remainder showing no difference. There were no studies that showed lower levels of vitamin C in organic potatoes or vegetables. Evidence for higher levels of vitamin C in organic produce was particularly strong for leafy vegetables. These also tended to have higher dry matter so that the higher levels might reflect the lower water content of organic produce. Lampkin (1990) also noted evidence for higher vitamin C levels in organic vegetables (28%) associated with higher dry matter values (23%), although yield was 24% lower for organic compared with conventionally grown produce. Lampkin emphasised the 12 year comparative study of Schupan (1975), which showed higher concentrations of protein, vitamin C, iron, potassium, calcium and phosphorus and lower levels of sodium in organic vegetables.

Worthington (1998) has evaluated 34 publications that have compared effects on the nutrient content of crops, of organic versus conventional management. As in the case of the Woese review, the author emphasised the mixed nature of the data. Some studies provided clear comparisons between organic and conventional farming, others examined combinations of farming practices and systems. Sampling sites included controlled research plots, working farms, storage facilities and retail outlets. The overall data for nitrates and individual vitamins, minerals and trace elements presented in this review are provided in summary form in Table 7.1. In general the findings support the overall conclusions drawn from the Woese review, and a number of the studies quoted are common to both. The clearest data were for nitrate levels which were higher, and vitamin C levels which were lower, in conventional compared with organic produce. Twenty five of 41 studies showed higher levels of nitrate and 21 of 36 studies showed lower levels of vitamin C. Data were insufficient or inconclusive for most of the other vitamins analysed. In the case of minerals and trace elements, levels found in organic produce tended to be either higher or the same as in conventional produce, with few studies showing lower levels in vegetables of organic origin.

Although there are serious limitations in the quantity and quality of the data described above, the careful reviews of both Woese (1997) and Worthington (1998), show a trend for fresh organic produce to have a higher nutrient concentration than conventional produce. Lampkin's review (1990) which

Table 7.1. Comparison of organic versus conventional growing methods on protein quality, nitrate, vitamin and mineral concentration of selected crops expressed to fresh weight. Modified from Worthington (1998)

Number of studies of organic crops shown to have increased, decreased or same nutrient content compared with conventionally grown crops:

Nutrient	Increased	Same	Decreased
Protein quality	3	0	0
Nitrate	5	10	25
Vitamin C	21	12	3
B-carotene	5	5	3
B vitamins	2	12	2
Calcium	21	20	6
Magnesium	17	24	4
Iron	15	14	6
Zinc	4	9	3

concluded favourably on the benefits of organic production, is however, much less comprehensive than these more recent publications and tends to be less objective in assessing the limitations of the studies conducted to date. Although the weight of evidence at the present time is suggestive of higher nutrient concentration in organic produce, this finding does not seem to apply to all nutrients or all crops, and further research of better quality than that currently available is needed to confirm these tentative conclusions. Some data may be explicable in terms of the reported higher water content of conventional crops. However if this were the major explanation, then a more consistent effect on levels of all the nutrients would be expected to be seen. The most consistent data are those available for vitamin C and nitrate which suggest beneficial effects of organic production on levels of these nutrients. It is possible that the two effects are related, since it is known that reaction between vitamin C and nitrate leads to depletion of vitamin C in human tissues.

7.2.2. Effects of agricultural methods on animal health

Mineral imbalances arising from unbalanced or excessive use of chemical fertilisers is a hazard that has long been known to affect the health of farm animals. In cattle, excessive levels of nitrogen or potassium in soil can lead to hypomagnesia in animals, resulting in grass tetany and poor reproductive performance; phosphorus excess is also associated with copper deficiency. However, few controlled intervention studies have compared effects of organic and conventionally grown feeds on animal health in the long term. Indeed, some of the quoted studies were originally conducted in the 1920s and 30s by scientists investigating 'essential growth factors' or vitamins. Table 7.2 summarises studies conducted between 1926 and 1992 that have assessed either weight or reproductive performance in groups of animals fed organic or

Table 7.2. Comparison of weight gain and reproductive performance in animals fed organic or conventionally grown feed

Species	Study	Animals fed organic feeds showed:
Hens/birds	McCarrison, 1926	Less % weight loss longer survival in polyneuritic bird
	Pfeiffer and Sabarth, 1932	Higher laying performance
	Plochberger, 1989	High egg and yolk weight
Rats and mice	McCarrison, 1926	Greater weight gain
	Pfeiffer, 1931	Lower mortality of young
	Rowlands and Wilkinson, 1930	Superior weight gain
	Scheunert *et al*, 1934	Shorter life span, worse health
	Miller and Dema, 1958	No difference in weight gain or reproduction
	Scott, 1960	Better reproduction in organic, worst performance in mixed organic/conventional feed
	McSheehy, 1977	No difference in weaning weight
	Neudecker, 1987; Velimirov *et al* 1992	No differences in gestation rate, litter weight or weaning weight. Lower still born/perinatal mortality
Rabbits	Hahn *et al*, 1971; Aehnelt and Hahn, 1973; Aehnelt and Hahn, 1978	Greater number of eggs, higher fertilisation rate
	Bram, 1974; Alter, 1978; Meinecke, 1982	No differences in reproductive performance, ovaries, uterus
	Gottschewski, 1975	Lower mortality of newborn
	Staiger, 1986	Long term fertility rate (3 generations) higher
	Edelmuller, 1984	More young born alive
Bulls	Aehnelt and Hahn, 1973	Better sperm motility

conventionally grown feed. Reproductive performance is generally considered a robust environmental health indicator because it is less affected by genetic determinants than other outcomes. Studies shown in table 7.2 have been divided according to species, with most data for rabbits.

Only one study (Scheunert *et al*,1934) observed worse performance in organically fed animals (rats), although Scott (1960) showed mice fed a mixed organic/conventional feed had poorer reproductive performance than those raised either on conventional or organic feed alone. Fifteen of the studies found that animals given organic feed fared better than those fed conventional feed. However there is little internal consistency even amongst the studies that have shown beneficial findings. Whereas some of the earlier studies in rabbits found clear evidence for reduced egg production and abnormal histology in conventionally fed animals (Hahn *et al*, 1971; Aehnelt and Hahn, 1973), others did not (Bram,1974; Alter, 1978; Meinecke, 1982). One of the criticisms of the earlier studies is that the nutrient compositions of the diets were frequently different between the two groups. Recent studies have provided more rigorously controlled nutrient conditions (Gottschewski, 1975; Edelmuller, 1984; Staiger, 1986). However even these have not demonstrated concordant findings, with some of the studies showing higher pregnancy and birth rates

(Staiger, 1986), whereas in others beneficial effects of organic feeds on numbers of live births were the dominant findings (Edelmuller, 1984). The more recent studies in rodents have also tended to observe greatest effects on numbers of still born animals and on perinatal mortality (Neudecker, 1987; Velimirov, 1992).

Based on the data available from controlled animal feeding studies, the evidence appears to be moderately strong to suggest that organic feed may have beneficial effects on animal health, particularly with respect to reproduction and pregnancy outcome. However the small number of studies, the variability in the study designs and the dated nature of much of the animal work suggest firm conclusions cannot be drawn at the present time. The lack of internal consistency in the data is of particular concern.

7.2.3. Effects of agricultural methods on human health

To date there have been no controlled studies to compare effects of organic and conventional products on human health. Such studies would pose considerable problems of feasibility, cost and ethics. They would need to be carried out under very carefully controlled conditions over long periods of time, thereby limiting the number and type of subjects who would be eligible and available for study. A few experiments from the 1930s and 1940s compared effects of foods produced using either organic or mixed (organic plus chemical) fertilisers. No effects were observed in experiments involving 260 adolescents (Wendt, 1943) or 300 adults (Reiter, 1938). In later studies, crops grown with mixed fertilisers were found to have more beta carotene and minerals but lower levels of B vitamins than crops grown organically. No effects of these products on blood parameters were observed in adults, although in infants there was a higher daily growth rate and higher serum beta carotene in children fed on crops grown under mixed fertiliser conditions (Dost and Schupan, 1944; Schupan, 1972). Lack of relevant dietary data, heterogeneity in the study populations and limited information on growing conditions means that much of this early data cannot be scrutinised according to current scientific criteria. For this reason no valuable inferences or interpretations can be derived from these studies.

7.3. Levels of protective antioxidants, anticancer agents, etc. in food

There is no reliable data at present to make a judgement as to whether the levels of antioxidants and related substances are comparable or different in conventional and organic grown foods.

7.4. Toxicological considerations

In section 7.2. we considered the relevant levels of nutrients (i.e. those substances that are necessary for life and growth) in conventionally and organically produced foods and how these affect health status in humans and animals. In this section consideration is given to possible adverse heath impacts from the consumption of anutrients (compounds with no direct nutritional value) in conventionally and organically grown foods. Effects on farm workers, food industry workers and on the environment are not assessed. Friends of the Earth, in their evidence to the House of Lords Committee on Organic Farming and the European Union (1999), make the statement "organic food does not contain pesticide and antibiotic residues, or as many chemical additives as conventional food. So not only is it safer, but this has been a major selling point addressing consumer concerns about these issues". At present, however, there is no reliable scientific evidence to demonstrate that the safety of organic foods to consumers is greater than the safety of conventionally produced food. It may be the case that the perception that organic food is healthier in itself provides health benefits. The analysis of the validity of this possibility is outside the scope of this chapter. In fact organic farmers do use natural pesticides and antibiotics.

To assess the safety of anutrients in food (including possible pesticide residues) it is necessary to discuss briefly the general principles of human reaction to them. Paracelceus identified, some four hundred years ago, that all substances have the capability to cause injury to living organisms provided the exposure level (dose) is sufficient. This original principle of toxicology has been confirmed many times since. The fundamental issue, in regard to non-nutrient chemicals in food, is what happens at lower exposure levels than those producing frank toxicity? It is widely accepted that for the great majority of chemicals there is a dose below which no evident toxic effect will occur. This is normally referred to as the "threshold dose" (Bridges and Bridges, 1996). A particular purpose of laboratory animal toxicity tests is to identify the threshold dose for each adverse effect. In practice, to avoid excessive use of animals and high costs, only a few exposure levels are employed in laboratory animal toxicity tests for an individual chemical. Consequently, the threshold dose may not be determined accurately and instead a "no observable adverse effect level" (NOAEL value) is identified. To allow for unreliability in this testing process and in the relevance of the findings to consumers, the NOAEL value is typically divided by a factor of 100 (the "safety" or "uncertainty" factor) to determine an acceptable (tolerable) daily intake value (ADI or TDI). This safety factor is intended to allow both for the fact that man might be more sensitive than laboratory animals (up to ten times more), and for a possible ten-fold variation in the response of individual members of the population to each chemical. As a next step, the ADI/TDI may be apportioned to various food items so that a "maximum residue limit" (MRL) is set for each common food item that may be contaminated. This MRL value provides a standard for determining the acceptability of that food item for human consumption. It is very likely that the great majority of the population is fully protected from significant adverse effects by the above approach.

There is considerable uncertainty as to whether a very small number of people could be affected chronically by residues approaching the MRL levels. Human epidemiological studies are unlikely to provide an answer to this question. Nonetheless, at levels substantially below the MRL even these very sensitive individuals are probably protected. Some individuals may be acutely ultra-sensitive to food components and show food intolerance or food allergy (hypersensitivity). These reactions, however, are generally due to natural macro-molecules such as complex natural proteins in the food (for example, ground nut protein), rather than to food additives or residues of pesticides or other low molecular weight chemicals (Danish Government, 2000). A survey in the USA of nearly 7000 self-proclaimed chemically ultra-sensitive individuals indicated that nearly half of them blamed pesticide exposure through agricultural or domestic use of pesticides for their condition (Ashford and Miller, 1991). Although it is uncertain whether these claims were justified, the survey provides evidence of public concern about adverse health effects of pesticide exposure.

Food items typically contain a very large number of components which are of no nutritional benefit (i.e. "anutrients"). These may be grouped into the following categories:

1. agrochemicals and fertilisers (e.g. nitrate), veterinary medicines (e.g. penicillin) and growth promoters (e.g. Lasalocid);
2. additions during "industrial" food processing,(e.g. food additives);
3. intrinsic anutrients. These are natural components of many foods, particularly common in broad leafed plants. They include both toxins and substances claimed to be anticarcinogenic and/or antioxidant. See Table 7.3 for examples.

Table 7.3. Intrinsic toxic anutrients and their major plant sources (Institute of Environmental April 1998)

Substance or group	Sources

Alkaloids
  Pyrrolizidine alkaloids
  Glycoalkaloids
	Many plants

Solanin, chaconine	Potatoes, yams
Cucurbitacins	Squash, marrow, courgette
Cyanogenic glycosides	Cassava, lima beans
Furocoumarins	Celery
Glycosinolates	Brassicas (cabbage, kale)
Hydrazine derivatives	
Agaritine	Cultivated mushrooms
Gyromitrin	False morels
Lathrogens	Chickpeas
Lectins	Legumes (red kidney beans)
Nitrate	Vegetables, especially lettuce, cabbage, spinach, potato, celery beetroot
Phytoestrogens	Legumes, soya
Protease inhibitors Trypsin inhibitors	Raw soya flour
Psoralens	Carrot, celery
Safrole	Sweet basil, nutmeg, cinnamon
Saponins	Legumes
Vasoactive amines	Cheese, wine, plantain, pineapple

4. adventitious products from food processing, including cooking and storage (e.g. polycyclic aromatic hydrocarbons);
5. environmental pollutants (e.g. dioxins);
6. microbial contamination products (e.g. mycotoxins).

Drinking water, beverages and indoor and ambient air also contain many thousands of trace components. Thus, typically humans are exposed to tens of thousands of chemicals daily. A considerable toxicological data base exists on synthetic pesticides, veterinary medicines, growth promoters and food additives. For many other anutrients in food, (especially the ones numbered (3) to (4) above) there is very limited or no information on possible adverse effects. As a consequence, we have a poor understanding of the toxicology of most natural foodstuffs. Nonetheless, it is evident that the human body has developed a number of defence mechanisms to cope with the continual exposure to a cocktail of anutrients. It seems that the great majority of the population has adequate defence mechanisms to cope with this assault providing exposure levels are kept "low". The relatively low levels of these anutrients mean that, with the exception of allergic reactions, acute (short-term) effects will not occur. There is no evidence that, in general, the body copes more effectively with "natural" anutrients than "synthetic" anutrients.

There is growing evidence that very low exposures to at least some anutrients may be protective against subsequent exposure to higher levels – a phenomenon termed "hormesis" (Calabrese and Baldwin, 1998). The generality of this phenomenon remains to be established. It may require a rethink about possible benefits from very low level exposures to such anutrients.

Health risks from any foods need to be set in the context. Since all our foods are derived from plants and animals they are neither intrinsically sterile nor free from unwanted substances (Danish Government, 2000). Producing a wide range of food items which are totally risk-free to all members of the population is probably an unattainable goal.

7.4.1. Safety of residues from synthetic agrochemicals

It is unlikely that significant differences will occur in the levels of the great majority of intrinsic anutrients between organically and conventionally produced foods. Moreover, organic food production cannot easily be protected from contamination by other airborne pollutants such as dioxins, polychlorinated biphenyls, heavy metals, etc. Thus, Woese *et al* (1997) have concluded, based on the published literature, that there are no differences in the heavy metal content of cereal and cereal products, potatoes or vegetables between organically produced and conventionally produced foods. It follows that the overall body load of anutrients ingested would be similar for people on comparable diets regardless of the source.

A recent study (Juhler *et al*, 1999) found no significant differences in human semen quality between farmers whose diet comprise either conventionally grown or organic food. To most individuals, the principal distinction between organic foods and conventional foods is the assumed absence of pesticide residues in organic foods. Kiraly (1996) stated that the toxicity of pesticides in food is much lower than the toxicity of natural components of food, based on his review of the literature. Ames *et al* (1990) reached a similar conclusion. In their investigation they concentrated on a group of plant anutrients which were classified as 'natural pesticides' and were produced in stressed, damaged or diseased plants. Their calculation was that Americans daily consume over 10,000 times more of these 'natural pesticides' than of synthetic pesticides. In animal studies where high doses of either 'natural' or synthetic pesticides were administered the long-term chronic toxicity profile was similar for both. This supports the view that 'natural' cannot be equated to 'safe'.

Critical questions are:
1. What are the relative levels of pesticides and other agrochemical and veterinary products in conventional and organic foods?
2. Are these levels of significance to human health?

Most Western governments have substantial monitoring programmes on residues of pesticides present in food. In the UK the programme is advised by the Working Party on Pesticide Residues (MAFF, 1998/99a). In its 1998 survey, over 90,000 tests were performed. Seventy-three percent of all food samples were found to be free of detectable residues and 26% (including all bread, milk and potato samples) were well below the maximum residue limit (MAFF, 1998/99a).The remaining 1% of the sample results were close to the MRL.

In many other EU member states the situation is rather similar. For example, in Denmark the levels of pesticides are well below the MRL in 98-99% of samples. For most test samples on conventionally grown fruit and vegetables pesticide residue cannot be detected even using the most sensitive available methodology. Where pesticides are detected typically the levels are around 1% or less of the ADI. It was estimated that in Denmark total intake of pesticides is about 200 micrograms per day per person and that the safety margin (i.e. ingestion level compared with the threshold dose) for intake of pesticides through foodstuff is greater than 1000. The levels of the majority of pesticides in food will be reduced substantially by food processing, including cooking, thereby increasing this safety margin. Although levels of pesticides in organic foods would be expected to be universally below the analytical detection limit, there has not been a comprehensive monitoring programme to confirm this. Of the occasional food samples with higher levels of pesticide the majority were imported into the EU. This is also the UK experience. Adverse effects are unlikely to occur from the occasional consumption of food items with levels of a pesticide which exceed the MRL. Nonetheless, such findings do highlight the need for continual vigilance and the targeting of food supply sources for which compliance with MRL standards is poor.

7.4.2. Residues arising from the use of materials approved for use in organic farming

The UK Soil Association has approved only the following pesticides for use in organic farming, namely:

- Copper ammonium carbonate/copper sulphate/copper oxychloride;
- Sulphur;

- Rotenone;
- Pyrethrum;
- Soft soap.

It is assumed that these pesticides will not leave residues in food. At present there is insufficient data to confirm this assumption. Indeed, it has been shown recently that rotenone (which is toxic to fish) does appear in low concentrations in the honey of bees treated with this natural insecticide (Jimenez *et al*, 2000). It is unclear from this study whether the rotenone contamination of the honey was direct or via absorption of rotenone by the bees. Pyrethrum residues have been found in brown tree snakes whose habitat has been treated with pyrethrum (Johnston *et al*, 1999). These data indicate that, under certain conditions at least, residues in food may arise from the use of natural pesticides. It is understood that copper is being phased out because of possible undesirable copper residues in treated foods.

7.4.3. Residues arising from the use of veterinary drugs and growth promoters

In conventional farming veterinary drugs are used widely to prevent, limit or cure disease in farm animals (Maxwell and Goddard, this volume). Drugs are also used in fish farming. Extensive regulation of their use occurs and veterinary residues are rarely detected in monitoring surveys. Thus, intake must be well below the ADI/MRL values (Brussaard *et al*, 1996; MAFF, 1998/99b; Danish Government Report, 2000). A selected, but diminishing number of drugs are also approved for use as growth promoters. Infrequently, values above the MRL, particularly for the sulphonamide drug sulfadimidine, have been found in meat samples. Occasional residues of this drug do not pose a risk to human health.

7.4.4. Residues arising from cross contamination by pesticides and veterinary products

Unintentional contamination of untreated raw food items can occur by a number of routes, for example airborne drift, contaminated water and contact with contaminated surfaces. It is, therefore, a challenge to ensure that many organic foods are indeed free of traces of pesticides and veterinary drugs.

Pesticides are commonly applied to crops using various spraying technologies. It is inevitable that some sprayed material will remain suspended in the air for sufficient time to be translocated some distance from the point of release (Haughton *et al*, 1998). Thus, organic crops may inadvertently become contaminated with trace amounts of pesticide. It may be the case that once analytical techniques are developed further, extremely low levels of pesticide will be detected in many organic foods.

Cross contamination in feed mills is a recognised problem. After preparation of a medicated feed it is common for subsequent batches of ostensibly drug-free meals to be contaminated with low concentrations of the original drug (Kennedy *et al*, 2000). Other means of cross contamination include use of the same vehicles for transporting medicated and non-medicated feeds. In a study in Northern Ireland of 161 feeds, declared by manufacturers to be free of drugs, half had quantifiable concentrations of antibiotics (Kennedy *et al*, 2000).

7.4.5. Microbial contamination products

Smith (2000) has drawn attention to the possibility of the growth of toxigenic fungi both during crop development and storage due to lack of usage of effective fungicides in organic farming. Potential risks include ergot disease and mycotoxin-induced immune system damage and cancer. Whether, in practice, there is a greater incidence of fungal toxins in organically grown foods than those grown and stored conventionally remains to be established.

7.5. The microbiological safety of conventional and organic food

7.5.1. Microbial changes

The massive impact of frequent food scares, particularly of microbial ones, provides powerful evidence favouring the view put forward by the German sociologist Ulrich Beck (1992) that we live in a "risk society." It is clear that many agree with his view that "in the past ... hazards could be traced back to an undersupply of hygienic technology. Today they have their basis in industrial overproduction. They are risks of modernization." The BSE crisis has provided as dramatic a supporting example as anyone could wish for. By recycling animal protein in feed to herbivores to increase production, a pathogen – the BSE agent – was unnaturally spread on a grand scale, with devastating consequences for the victims of variant CJD, cattle, farmers, taxpayers, and public confidence in our food safety systems. Another very powerful example is provided by the chicken industry. In essence, its phenomenal growth has only been made possible by procedures with principles about as different from those of the organic movement as one could imagine. In 1934 the US broiler industry (Boyd and Watts, 1997) produced 34 million birds, with per capita consumption of 0.7 pounds. By 1994 production had soared to 7,018 million birds and per capita consumption almost a hundred-fold to 69.9 pounds. All these changes were made possible by the application of "big science" – massive breeding programmes, year-round confinement (made possible by the discovery of vitamin D in 1926) the development of high-performance rations, and microbial disease control by antibiotics and vaccines. But the confinement of birds at high density and the ever-increasing commercial pressure to increase line speeds in mechanised slaughter houses (together with the dominance of the industry by a very small number of breeders) provided ideal opportunities for the spread of microorganisms in flocks and their further dissemination by carcase cross-contamination. *Salmonella* has been a major beneficiary in the past.

To understand and control *Salmonella* we can draw on knowledge about the organism that has been accumulating for about a century. However, this is not the case for the other important food-borne bacteria. Thus techniques for detecting *Campylobacter*, the commonest cause of bacterial gastrointestinal disease in the UK, were only established in 1977. *E.coli* O157, much rarer but much more likely to cause lethal infections or ones which permanently cripple by causing kidney and brain damage, is a newly emerging pathogen. It first appeared in England in 1983, in Scotland in 1984 and Northern Ireland in 1989. The overwhelming majority of human cases of *Campylobacter* are sporadic and never tracked to a source. Milk-borne outbreaks occur from time to time. The organism is common in wild birds; although broiler chickens are often contaminated, the proportion of cases due to their consumption is uncertain. In contrast, *E.coli* O157 has a propensity to cause dramatic outbreaks. It is clear that the main reservoir of the organism is the gastrointestinal tract of farm animals – usually cattle – in which it resides as a normal member of the microbial flora without causing disease. Transmission to man is via manure – either in food (meat, milk, vegetables) via contaminated drinking water, or directly from the environment or from other human cases by the faecal-oral route. A classic outbreak which showed the versatility and nastiness of this pathogen occurred in a rural town in Maine, USA, in 1992 (Cieslak *et al,* 1993). The index case was a 39 year old lacto-ovo-vegetarian whose diet was almost exclusively made up of vegetables from her garden, fertilized by manure from a cow and calf kept to produce the latter. Almost certainly she became infected by eating inadequately washed garden produce. Three other cases occurred in children a few days later – probably infected by the person-to-person route. A two-year old developed the haemolytic uraemic syndrome (affecting the kidneys and the blood – a well known complication of *E.coli* O157 infection) and died.

Insufficient data on the degree of contamination of organic and conventionally grown foods by *Campylobacter*, *E.coli* O157 and *Salmonella* exists to allow comparison between the levels that can be ascribed to different farming methods. The natural history of *Campylobacter* is so poorly understood that even raising hypotheses about the likelihood of differences occurring is not profitable at this time. For *E.coli* O157, however, a number of studies have investigated the effect of different cattle management factors on the prevalence of the organism in herds (Hancock *et al*, 1998). Differences in herd size, feeding practices, or the patterns of manure use do not show any important consistent correlations with its occurrence. No studies on organic systems have yet been reported, though studies are continuing. The question has also been raised as to the role played by farming practices in the origin of *E.coli* O157. The microbiological evidence of its novelty as a human pathogen is very strong. It had never been isolated anywhere before the late 1970's. But where and when it evolved, and why it emerged as a virulent pathogen for man – an occasional host – but as a harmless gut resident in its animal hosts is not known. Its antibiotic sensitivity patterns indicate that antibiotic use had nothing to do with its origins. It is clear, however, that its main virulence factors have been acquired by horizontal gene exchange from other organisms. Speculation that it – or a close relative – might have originated in cattle on the Argentinian pampas has been engendered by the observation that the haemolytic uraemic syndrome is much commoner in children in that country that anywhere else in the world, and has been a significant medical problem there since the 1960's (Lopez *et al*, 1998).

The nastiness and newness of *E.coli* O157 raises in acute form questions about the risk posed to human health by the application of faeces and sewage sludge to agricultural land, and whether current UK Codes of Practice are appropriate for the control of this new organism. A crucial uncertainty is whether its survival time on soil is longer than that of traditional enteric pathogens, on which the Codes of

Practice are based. Research is in progress to answer this question (Fenlon *et al*, 2000). Although organic farming in the UK accounts for only a small fraction of manure applied to the land (relatively recent estimates indicate a total annual deposition of 2.1 x 10^7 t dry weight of animal wastes and 1.13 x 10^8 t wet weight of faeces from grazing animals) its dependence on manure makes this a pressing problem for organic farmers. The heat of composting can accelerate the death of pathogens, and work is in progress to investigate the parameters of this for *E.coli* O157.

Foodborne microbial infections are common (in 1999 in England and Wales there were 54,994, 17,251 and 1084 laboratory-confirmed cases of infection with *Campylobacter, Salmonella* and *E.coli* O157 respectively) whereas pesticide intoxications are not; virtually none of the many enquiries made to the UK poisons centres (7,031 to the Scottish Poisons Information Bureau in 1998, (Good and Bateman, 1999)) are about the latter. Any claims that organic foods are healthier than those produced conventionally must be assessed in the light of these facts. For red meat and vegetables there is no evidence that either production system is superior from the microbial safety point of view. Intuitively it could be supposed that the organic emphasis on the use of animal manures, encouragement of biological cycles involving microorganisms, and maintenance of biodiversity might enhance the occurrence of organisms such as *E.coli* O157 in animals and favour their occurrence in the environment and on food crops. Until the data has been collected to confirm or refute these notions the conclusion must be firmly drawn that from the microbiological standpoint organic foods have – at best – no safety advantage. It follows that producers, processors, vendors and consumers of both organic and conventional products must apply good hygiene practice and measures such as the Hazard Analysis and Critical Control Point system (HACCP) (Pennington, 1997).

7.5.2. Milk pasteurisation

On a historical as well as a contemporary note the pasteurization of milk has a particular relevance here for the organic movement. It was vigorously opposed by organic farming pioneers such as Lady Eve Balfour (Balfour, 1948) and has been recently resisted as a compulsory measure by the Soil Association on the grounds of consumer choice (Soil Association, 1998). However, the emergence of *E.coli* O157 in the last decade as a pathogen capable of causing permanent kidney and brain damage and killing young children, and the occurrence of such outbreaks due to the consumption of milk that is unpasteurized or contaminated after pasteurization (Pennington, 2000) has made it impossible to resist this as an essential measure to protect public health.

7.6. Conclusions

1. Food is a highly complex medium. In addition to macro and micronutrients, typically food items contain small amounts of many components (anutrients) of no nutritional value to consumers. The health benefits and risks of a particular food item depend on the genetic and environmental status of the individual consuming the food and on the ability to absorb (bioavailability) many of the components it contains.

2. There have been very few scientific studies in which foods grown conventionally have been compared, under similar conditions, with those produced organically, in terms of their chemical composition or their biological effects on the consuming organism. It would appear, however, that typically no differences can be demonstrated and where differences are detected they are very small.

3. Some studies have shown slightly enhanced levels of certain micronutrients, eg: vitamin content, in organic foods compared with foods grown conventionally. In part this may be ascribed to higher water content in some conventional foods. It is very unlikely that such small differences in nutrient content would have health implications for consumers except possibly for individuals with a particular micronutrient deficiency.

4. Animal studies that have been conducted to compare health effects of conventionally and organically grown produce are very limited in number and have involved only a few species. Although some studies are suggestive of superior reproductive outcomes in organically fed animals, the limitations in the study designs and lack of internal consistency in the findings mean that they are of limited value in providing a scientific basis for evaluating health effects of organic foods.

5. Anutrients in food come from many sources; the majority of these sources are natural. It has been calculated that the level of natural anutrients is of the order of 10,000 times greater than synthetic contaminants in conventional foods. A critical question is whether each anutrient occurs at levels below the threshold for its toxicity. In raw foods only pesticide and veterinary drug residues may be expected to be higher in conventional foods compared with organic foods. Extensive evidence shows, however, that the levels of these components are well below the relevant threshold for adverse effects in the great majority of foods sampled. For nearly all consumers it can be concluded that there is no health risk from ingesting food with levels of pesticides and veterinary drugs currently found in the UK.

6. It is likely that inadvertent contamination of organic foods with certain pesticides and veterinary drugs will occur, unless rigorous preventative measures are used. Although there are no health implications from such cross contamination, it defeats one of the objectives of organic food producers.

7. It may be argued that because of the very restricted use of pesticides and antibiotics in organic food production and the greater use of natural fertilisers and manures there is a potentially higher risk of contamination by microorganisms (bacteria and/or fungi). There is limited evidence to support this in practice. However, the commitment of organic farmers to control every stage of the food production process may well ameliorate this problem.

8. Based on our current limited scientific knowledge, it appears that the widely held view of the public that organic foods are safer and healthier than conventional foods is incorrect for the great majority of consumers.

References

Aehnelt E. and Hahn, J. (1978) Animal fertility: a possibility for biological quality assay of fodder and feeds. *Bio-Dynamics*, **25**, 36-47.

Aehnelt, E. and Hahn, J. (1973) Fruchbarkeit der Tiere-eine Moglichkeit zur biologischen Qualitatsprufung von Futter und Nahrungsmitteln? *Tieraztl Umsch*, **28**, 155-160.

Alter, G. (1978) *Uber den Einfluß von Futterungsfaktoren auf das ruchtbarkeitsgeschehen, den Ascorbinsauregehalt und den histologischen Aufbau der Ovarien von weiblichen Kaninchen.* Dissertation. Tierarztliche Hochschule Hannover, Germany.

Ames, B.N., Profet, M. and Swirsky-Gold, L. (1990) Dietary pesticides (99.99%) all natural *Proc. Nat. Acad. Sci, USA*, **87**, 7777-7781.

Ashford, N.A. and Miller C.S. (1991) *Chemical exposures: low levels and high stakes.* Van Nostrand Reinhold, New York.

Balfour, E.B. (1948) *The living soil: evidence of the importance to human health of soil vitality, with special reference to post-war planning* (8th ed.), Faber and Faber, London.

Beck U (1992) *Risk society. Towards a new modernity* (translated by M. Ritter). Sage, London p21.

Boyd, W. and Watts, M. (1997) Agro industrial just-in-time. The chicken industry and post-war American capitalism. In: *Globalising food* (Eds. D. Goodman and M.J. Watts). Routledge, London, pp 192-225.

Bram, L. (1974) *Uber den Einfluß von Futterungsfaktoren auf den Ascorbinsauregehalt und den histologischen Aufbau der Nebennieren von weiblichen Kaninchen unter besonderer Berucksichtigung der Beziehungen zwischen Nebennierenfunktion und Fruchtbarkeit.* Dissertation. Tierarzliche Hochschule Hannover, Germany.

Bridges, J.W. and Bridges, O. (1996) Hazards of growth promoting agents and strategies of risk assessment. In: *Proceedings of Growth Promoters and Beef Production Conference*, Brussels. EU publications.

Brussaard, J,H, Van Dokkum, W., Van der Paauw, G.G., De Vos, R.H., De Kort, W.L., Lowik, M.R. (1996) Dietary intake of food contaminants in The Netherlands (Dutch Nutrition Surveillance System) *Food Additives and Contaminants* **1(5)**, 561-573.

Calabrese, E.J. and Baldwin, L.A. (1998) Can the concept of hormesis be generalised to carcinogenesis? *Regul. Toxicol. Pharmacol*, **28**, 230-241.

Cieslack, P.R., Barrett, T.J., Griffin, P.M., Gensheiner, K.F., Beckett, G., Buffington, J. and Smith, M.J. (1993) *E.coli* O157:H7 infection from a manured garden. *Lancet*, **342**, 367.

Daldy, Y, (1940) Food production without artificial fertilisers. *Nature*, **145,** 905-906.

Danish Government (2000) *Denmark: top priority on food safety.* Danish Veterinary and Food Administration, Soborg.

Dost, F.H. and Schupan, W. (1944) Uber Ernahrungsversuche mit verschieden gedungten Gemusen. III. Teil. *Ernaehrung (Leipzig), 9, 581-586.*

Edelmuller, I. (1984) *Untersuchungen zur Qualitatserfassung von Produkten aus unterschiedlichen Anbausystemen (biologisch-dynamisch bzw. Konventionell) mittels. Futerungsversuchen an Kaninchen.* Dissertation, University of Vienna, Austria.

Fenlon, D.R., Ogden, I.D., Vinten, A. and Svoboda, I. (2000) The fate of *Escherichia coli* and *E.coli* O157 in cattle slurry after application to land. *Journal of Applied Microbiology Supplement*, **88**, 1495-1565.

Good, A.M. and Bateman, D.N. (1999) Chemicals as a Public Health issue: enquiries to the Scottish Poisons Information Bureau. *SCIEH Weekly Report* (Scottish Centre for Infection and Environmental Health) 33, 70-72.

Gottschewski, G.H.M. (1975) Neue Moglichkeiten zur großeren Effizienz der toxikologischen Prufung von Pestiziden, Ruckstanden und Herbiziden. *Qual Plant Plant Foods Hum Nutr*, **25**, 21-42.

Hahn. J., Aehnelt, E., Grunert, E., Schiller, H., Lengauer, E., Schulz, L-Cl. and Pohlenz, J. (1971) Uterus-und Ovarbefunde bei Kaninchen nach Futterung mit Heu von ungedungtem und intensiv gedungtem Grunland. *Deutsch Eieraeztl Wochenschr*, **78**, 114-118.

Hancock, D.D., Besser, T.E., and Rue, D.H. (1998) Ecology of *Escherichia coli* O157:H7 in cattle and impact of management practises. In*: Escherichia coli O157:H7 and other Shiga Toxin-Producing E.coli strains* (Eds. J.B. Kaper, and A.D. O'Brien). ASM Press, Washington, DC, pp 85-91.

Haughton, A.J., Wilcox, A., Chaney, K., Cooper, S.E. and Boatman, N.D. (1998) Spray drift into field margins: the effect of width of buffer strip and plant species on the interception of spray drift. *Brighton Crop Protection Conference: Pests and Diseases, Volume 1*: British Crop Protection Council, Farnham pp 285-290.

House of Lords (1999) House of Lords Select Committee on European Communities Report (16th Report). *Organic farming and the European Union.* Stationery Office, London.

Institute of Environmental Health (1998) Report for MAFF, unpublished, Leicester.

Jimenez, J.J., Bernal, J.L., del Nozal, M.J., Novo, M., Higes, M. and Llorente, J. (2000) Determination of rotenone residues in raw honey by solid-phase extraction and high performance liquid chromatography. *Journal of Chromatography A*, **871**, 67-73

Johnston, J.J., Furcolow, C.A., Voltz, S.A., Mauldin, R.E., Primus, T.M., Savarie, P.J. and Brooks, J.E. (1999) Quantification of pyrethrum residues in brown tree snakes. *Journal of Chromotographic Science*, **37(1)**: 5-10.

Juhler, R.R., Larsen, S.B., Meyer, O., Jensen, N.D., Spano, M., Giwercman, A. and Bonde, J.P. (1999) Human semen quality in relation to dietary pesticide exposure and organic diet. *Archives of Environmental Contamination and Toxicology*, **37**, 415-423

Kennedy, D.G., Canaan, A. and McCracken, R.J. (2000) Regulatory problems caused by contamination, a frequently overlooked cause of veterinary drug residues. *Journal of Chromatography A*, **882**, 37-52.

Kiraly, Z. (1996) Sustainable agriculture and the use of pesticides. *Journal of Environmental Science and Health Part B*, **31(3)**, 283-291.

Lampkin, N. (1990) The wider issues. In: *Organic Farming* (Ed. N. Lampkin). Farming Press, Ipswich pp 557-611.

Lopez, E.L., Contrini, M.M. and De Rosa, M.F. 1998. *Epidemiology of Shiga Toxin-producing Escherichia coli in South America*. (Eds. J.B. Kaper, J.B. and A.D. O'Brien). ASM Press, Washington, DC pp 30-37.

MAFF (1998/99) *Annual Report of the Working Party on Pesticide Residues*. Ministry of Agriculture, Fisheries and Food, London.

MAFF (1998/99) *Annual Report of the Working Party on Veterinary Residues*. Ministry of Agriculture, Fisheries and Food, London.

McCarrison, R. (1926) The effect of manurial conditions on the nutritive and vitamin values of millet and wheat. *Indian J. Med. Res.*, **14**, 351-378.

McSheehy, T W. (1977) Nutritive value of wheat grown under organic and chemical systems of farming. *Qualitas Planitarum*, 27, 113-123.

Meinecke B. (1982) Untersuchungen zur Wirkung intensiv min- eratisch gediingten Futters auf die Fruchtbarkeit des Kanin chens. *Zentralbl Veterinaermed 29*, 5-15.

Miller, D.S. and Dema, I.S. (1958) Nutritive value of wheat from the Rothamsted Broadbalk field. *Proc. Nutr. Soc., 17*, xliv-xlv.

Neudecker C, (1987) Diingung und Qualitdt yon Lebensmitteln-Tierfijtterungsversuche mit mineralisch und organisch gediingten Kartoffeln und Mbbren. In: *Land- baumethoden und Nahrungsqualitiit (Materialien und Berichte Nr 60)* Akademie filr Politische Bildung, Tutzing, Germany, pp 110-125.

Pennington, T.H. (1997) *The Pennington Group Report on the circumstances leading to the 1996 outbreak of infection with E.coli O157 in Scotland, the implications for food safety, and the lessons to be learned*. The Stationery Office. Edinburgh.

Pennington, T.H. (2000) VTEC: lessons learned from British oubreaks. *Journal of Applied Microbiology Supplement*, **88**, 905-985.

Pfeiffer, E. (1931) Vergicichender Fdtterungsversuch mit min- Oleralisch gedfingtern ur..'- biologisch-dynamisch gediingtern Getreide. *Demeter, 6*, 87-89.

Pfeiffer, E. and Sabarth, E. (1932) Vergleichender Fiitterungsversuch mit Hiihnern. *Demeter, 7*,198-200.

Plochberger, K. (1989) Feeding experiments. A criterion for quality estimation of biologically and conventionally produced foods. *Agric Ecosyst Etiviron, 27*, 419-428.

Reiter, H., Ertel, H., Wendt, H., Pies Prufer, J., Barth, L., Schroder, H., Catel, W., Dost, F.H. and Scheunert, A. (1938) Uber Ernahrungsversuche mit verscieden gedungten Gemusen. *Ernaehrung (Leipzeg)*, **3**, 53-69.

Rowlands, M.J. and Wilkinson, B. (1930) Vitamin B content of grass reeds in relation to manures. *Biochem J*, **24**, 199-204.

Scheunert, A., Sachne, M. and Speche, R. (1934) Uber die Wirkung fortgesetzter Verfutterung von Nahrungsmitteln, die mit und ohne kunstlichen Dunger gezogen sind. *Biochem Z*, **274**, 372-396.

Schupan, W. (1972) Effects of the application of inorganic and organic manures on the market quality and on the biological value of agricultural produce. *Qualitas Planitarum*, **21**, 381-398.

Schupan, W. (1975) Yield maximisation versus biological value. *Qualitas Planitarum*, **24**, 281-310.

Scott, P.P., Greaves, J.P. and Scott, M.G. (1960) Reproduction in laboratory animals as a measure of the value of some natural and processed foods. *J. Reprod Fertil*, **1**, 130-138.

Smith, J. (2000) Now it's a bugs life. *Glasgow Herald* Saturday Magazine, 22nd July, p19-21.

Soil Association (1998) *Government consultation on the proposed ban on raw cows' drinking milk: draft submission*. Soil Association, Bristol.

Staiger, D. (1986) *Einfluße konventionell und biologischedynamisch angebauten Futters auf Fruchbarkeit, allgemeinen Gesundheitszustand und Fleischqualitat beim Hauskaninchen*. Dissertation, Rheinische FriedrichWilhelms-Universitate, Bonn, Germany.

Velimirov, A., Plochberger, K., Huspeka, U. and Schott, W. (1992) The influence of biologically and conventionally cultivated food on the fertility of rats. *Biol. Agric. Hort.*, **8**, 325-337.

Wendt, H. (1943) Uber einen langjahrigen Ernahrungsversuch am Menschen mit verschieden gedungten Gemusen und Kartoffeln. *Ernaehrung (Leipzig)*, **8**, 281-295.

Woese, K., Lange, D., Boess, C. and Bogl, K.W. (1997) A comparison of organically and conventionally grown foods – results of a review of the relevant literature. *Journal of Sci. Food Agriculture*, **74**, 281-293.

Worthington, V. (1998) Effect of agricultural methods on nutritional quality: a comparison of organic with conventional crops. *Alternative Therapies*, **4**, 58-69.

Chapter Eight

Conclusion

Dr P B Tinker OBE, MA, PhD, DSc, FIBiol, FRSC, FRAgS

8.1 Conclusion

The frequently contentious information reviewed in this book about the different farming systems has to be brought to a conclusion. This is organised in terms of benefits (or the reverse) to the Consumer, to the Environment, to Ethics, to Farmers and to the Rural Community. All of these may combine into a net advantage or disadvantage for the country, food consumers, and the rural population.

8.2 Advantages to the consumer

8.2.1 Food quality

This is a very ill-defined concept (Lampkin, 1990, p558). Taste and appearance are personal assessments, and ultimately the individual consumers will have to determine this themselves. If they prefer either organic or conventionally grown food on the basis of their own experience, that is the right of the consumer, and their preference will register in the markets - it is not a scientific issue. Williams *et al* (see this volume, sections 7.1-7.3) shows that there are very few consistent differences in nutritional quality between organic and conventional food, that there is surprisingly little evidence on the subject, that some of the research is suspect and that results are often indefinite or conflicting. Organic food may contain a higher dry matter level, as expected from the expected differences in nitrogen supply and growth rate of organic crops. In general this carries no health or nutritional implications. Organic food can also contain a higher percentage of nitrate and vitamin C, possibly associated with the higher percentage of dry matter. Otherwise there is no evidence for consistent differences, and in total, there appears to be no good basis for the claim that organic food is of higher quality in its composition.

8.2.2. Health implications - toxicity

This could arise from agrochemical (insecticides, fungicides, herbicides, growth regulators, antibiotics) spray residues, or nitrate. The risk from spray residues should be controllable, though earlier work showed a lower appearance of residues in organic food (Lampkin, 1990). The materials used as pesticides can be analysed for at extremely small concentrations, and the acceptable levels in food are defined by the MAFF or now the Food Standards Agency, with a large safety margin (see Williams *et al*, section 7.4.). Thus any level of dependability and safety could be obtained by increasing the intensity of the chemical testing routine for residues in produce. In fact residues in excess of the defined acceptable levels are found very rarely (see Williams *et al*, Section 7.4, this volume). As the sensitivity of the chemical techniques is increased, so it will become possible to find a tiny amount of almost any chemical in all foods. At this level, total lack of "contamination" is not possible.

Nitrate in water and in food has been blamed for some health dangers, but the evidence of medical hazards is weak, and there may also be beneficial functions of nitrate in humans (Wilson *et al*, 1999). Plants with high nitrate levels can be produced with both fertilisers and organic manures, but the control of nitrogen supply to the plant with the latter is less precise (see Greenland, this volume). Nitrate could be closely and regularly monitored in food if it is genuinely believed to be a hazard.

8.2.3 Health implications - microbiology

The second health aspect is the possibility of microbiological contamination (see Williams *et al*, Section 7.5, this volume). Microbial infections are far more common than toxic substance problems. They can arise from industrial processes in handling and slaughter, or microbes in soil or animal manures used for growing food crops, such as *E. coli* O157, that can cause outbreaks of serious disease through infected produce or milk. This and some other pathogens come from the wastes of farm animals. These are most likely to be found on food where animal manures are a major part of the agronomic system, which is most likely in organic farming. In addition, there are more specific problems arising from infection of animal products, such as *Salmonella* on poultry products, that arises as a result of mass production methods with low standards. The latter are against UKROFS rules, and are rarer under any system now, as standards are tightened up. The BSE epidemic resulted from recycling of animal tissues into the feed, not microbial contamination. This problem hardly affected organic farmers, as their principles prevented such recycling. However, the general conclusion (see Williams *et al,* section 7.5) is that microbiological health hazards are more important than toxicological dangers, and that the former may be more likely to occur in organic than in conventional farming, though there are no good data yet.

The conclusion of the whole chapter on food quality and safety aspects (see Williams *et al*, section 7.6) is that there is no clear basis for the statement that organic food is better for the consumer than conventionally grown food.

8.2.4. The price of food

Consumers will tend to purchase the cheapest food unless they believe that they gain some benefit from a more expensive product, or if they see it as a status symbol. In high-income households the price difference will have little impact; but in households with lower budgets it will be important. As the organic market grows, it may affect more consumers on modest incomes, where the actual benefits obtained for the premium price will be more carefully considered. At present food grown by conventional or integrated farming systems is the cheapest, but it is possible that food from integrated farming will be sold at a small premium to conventional produce once significant brands are established. The premium for organic food is now considerable (see Colman, this volume), but this is not justifiable on a strictly scientific assessment of food quality, from the evidence reviewed here, though it does reflect higher production costs. Part of the premium might be justified in terms of environmental gains. Everything depends upon the customers' perception of direct benefits to themselves and their families, and their wish to support environmental gains. At present it appears that the number of consumers prepared to pay the premium is increasing steadily.

8.3. Advantages to the environment

8.3.1. Soil quality

Greenland (see this volume) shows that the only real difference following from organic conversion is a larger percentage of organic matter in the soil, and possibly larger populations of earthworms (see Greenwood, this volume). This certainly has some advantages in principle, but the differences to be expected in practice will seldom give a significant advantage to the farmer or the environment in the UK. It is a factor that needs to be taken into account in rather specialised situations. On the other hand the fertility of the soil (the level of plant nutrients) may be declining under an organic regime, where it is more difficult to replace phosphorus and potassium. If so, the reserves laid down in the soil by fertilising over many years may gradually be exhausted. In total one cannot say that 'soil quality' is necessarily higher under organic farming than under a sensible conventional or integrated regime.

8.3.2. Wildlife and biodiversity

On average the practices of organic farming, including the omission of all synthetic biocides, appears to lead to significantly larger populations of some wildlife species and to higher biodiversity than in conventional systems. The level of information is still too scanty to be certain of the effects in specific situations. Apart from the use of biocides, wildlife enhancement depends upon the actions of the individual farmer, such as more woodlands, wider hedges, wildlife corridors, field margins, and beetle banks,. These are specifically encouraged both in organic and integrated farming,, but could be used just as much in any of the Farming Systems if the farmer so wished, or was paid to do. The important question now is to determine if integrated systems, with restricted use of biocides, can be managed to give results that are similar to those with organic farming.

8.3.3. Landscape appearance

This is largely a personal and emotional matter. The features that attract those who love the traditional appearance of the landscape do not depend upon organic farming as such, but upon certain desirable features such as much grassland with grazing stock, and moderate-sized fields with bushy hedges, plenty of trees and diverse and plentiful wildlife. Some issues are hardly agricultural at all, such as type and density of housing. All these can be encouraged by incentives to farmers, as in Environmentally Sensitive Areas, or by changed planning arrangements. Such schemes could be extended, in a general transfer of subsidies from supporting the production of surpluses to supporting environmental gains. At present both organic and integrated farmers aim to increase and retain these attractive features, and all farmers are coming to recognise that landscape is a great advantage that can benefit tourism and other alternative enterprises.

8.4 Ethical advantages

8.4.1. Stock management

The level of concern for farm animals is now very high. Non-vegetarians are prepared to eat meat, but do not want to think of animals being ill-treated to supply this demand. The present UKROFS regulations, LEAF guidelines or RSPCA Freedom Foods Standard rules would be supported by the great majority of the rural and urban populations. An important lead was provided in this by organic farming, but the same rules can and should be adopted by any farmer, without serious damage to his enterprise. However, some of the organic rules may cause problems in the health of animals (see Maxwell, this volume).

8.4.2. Sustainability

Almost any form of agriculture is of course more sustainable than most other industries, because it produces a net energy gain. None of the systems discussed here, if used responsibly, will damage the productive capacity of the soil. It is often suggested that conventional agriculture is unsustainable because it uses non-replaceable resources such as oil and fertiliser raw materials to produce fertilisers and pesticides. However, the production and use of all farm machinery is non-sustainable in this sense, yet all forms of modern agriculture use machinery, and use phosphate and potassium rocks (latest estimates are that at present rates of use phosphate rocks will last over 100 years, and potassium rocks over 1000). The major difference lies in the use of synthetic nitrogen fertilisers. The production of these liberates carbon dioxide, but on the other hand the nitrogen fertiliser leads to more fixation of carbon dioxide in crops. Since it is impossible to visualise organic farming feeding the world in the realisable future, it is not an issue in terms of global sustainability. It seems naive to worry about the small differences between the sustainability of conventional, integrated or organic systems, while the global community wastes far more non-replaceable resources on leisure pursuits, large motor cars, and other optional extras. Sustainability does not seem to be a real issue in this debate

8.5 Advantages to the farmer

8.5.1. Economic benefits

At present it seems that the constant downwards pressure on agricultural prices grown by conventional and integrated methods is not affecting organic systems so much, so that premiums remain stable, or may even increase (see Colman, this volume). There is consequently a growing tendency to convert to organic farming, and this may be seen as one of the few profitable 'new crops' available to UK farmers at present. The fact that some UK farmers can sell less food for more money is at present quite helpful to agriculture. It is of course astonishing that the UK should import such a large fraction of its organic requirements at present, and it is clearly advantageous to UK agriculture for it to increase its share of the UK market. The long conversion process is the main handicap.

In the longer term the future of organic farming depends upon the popular belief that the produce is superior. The move to Farm Assurance and integrated farming systems is being driven by the retailers, and this will gradually lessen the differences between organic and other farming methods, to the point where the only differentiation may lie in the use of synthetic chemicals. The obvious danger is that perceptions may change, if indeed there is no scientifically identifiable superiority in the quality of the produce or the environmental gain, and that many organic farms may have to go back to conventional farming. An economic recession might have the same effect.

8.5.2. Effects on management of farms

It would be expected that organic farming would be more difficult and call for more careful judgements, because of the need to control weed infestations and plant diseases (see Plumb, this volume), animal diseases (Maxwell, this volume), and the nutrient cycle (see Greenland, this volume) with fewer direct tools than are available to a conventional farmer. Decisions will be longer term and more complex, and farming skill will be at a premium. Fertiliser nitrogen is immediately soluble and absorbable, whereas farmyard manure has to break down through complex weather-dependent processes to produce nitrate and ammonium ions. Equally, the judgement on when to call in conventional medicines for sick animals – which temporarily lose their organic status – must often be difficult. It is important to remember the range in skill and efficiency between individual farmers, and that range is possibly greatest for organic systems. The interest in accurate management is best expressed in the concepts of Precision Farming, and it seems likely that these will be easiest to apply on conventional farms.

8.5.3. Effects on the rural community

The rural community is supported by a thriving agriculture. If a fraction of farmers can make a better living by organic production, this is beneficial, and their lower yields will reduce oversupply to the market, and thereby tend to stabilise it. However, if at some stage organic demand should decrease, there could be a period in which organic farmers might switch back to conventional farming and try to maintain their incomes by higher production levels. A stable balance between the systems is the best situation. It is to be hoped that the whole farming community will get more financial support for improvements to the landscape and to wildlife, and this will help to stabilise the situation.

8.6 Final conclusion

The most likely trend over the next few years is that the UK market for organic produce will continue to increase. However, there have been fluctuations in this market before, and major changes in the national economy, the subsidy structure of the agricultural industry or the organic subsection of the latter could affect this trend, positively or negatively

The most interesting scientific question at present is how far integrated farming can deliver the best aspects of both conventional and organic systems. Undoubtedly conventional farming has caused damage to wildlife and landscape, though this is gradually being diminished. On the other side, some organic farming ideas seem quite unscientific, such as distinguishing between crude potassium-containing rocks (that are acceptable) and potassium chloride that has been re-crystallised in water (that is not). Ideas on limiting biocides are sensible, but it is even more so to seek for safer and more specific chemicals, and this will not happen if all synthetic pesticides are banned. The future appears to lie in working towards a compromise, taking the best parts of each farming system. That compromise will be some form of integrated farming, but there is still much work to do in determining what this really means in terms of acceptable and efficient procedures.

Finally, it has been surprising to find how many subject areas are deficient in good research results. It is clear that some organisation should arrange to fill these gaps.

References

Lampkin, N. (1990) *Organic Farming*. 1994 version. Farming Press, Tonbridge, UK.
Wilson, W., Ball, A S. and Hinton, R.H. (eds) (1999). *Managing risks of nitrates to humans and the environment*. Royal Society of Chemistry, London.

Biographies

Professor Jim Bridges

Jim Bridges is Professor of Toxicology at the University of Surrey. His main research interest is the risk assessment of chemicals in food and the environment. He has published over 300 research papers and reviews. Prof Bridges is the Chairman of the EU Scientific Advisory Committee of Toxicology, Ecotoxicology and the Environment, a member of the EU Scientific Steering Committee (the EU lead Committee on Public Health) and Chairman of the EU Working Party on the Harmonisation of Risk Assessment. In the UK he has served on many Committees, including the Veterinary Products Committee, the Novel and Irradiated Foods Committee and the HSE WATCH Committee. He was a founder member and past President of the British Toxicological Society.

Dr Olga Bridges

Olga Bridges is a lecturer in Environmental Health at the University of Surrey. Her principal current research interest is health risk communication. She has recently conducted a study of risk ranking of food related factors as viewed by food scientists from different European countries and different disciplines. Dr Bridges has published widely on the impact of environmental factors on human health in the Russian Federation. She is Director of the University's BSc in Public and Environmental Health.

Professor David Colman

David Colman is Professor of Agricultural Economics at the University of Manchester, and is Director of the Farm Business survey for the North-West of England. He is Vice-President of the International Association of Agricultural Economists and a past President of the Agricultural Economics Society in the UK. He has acted as expert advisor to the House of Commons Agriculture Committee on a two occasions in relation to the dairy sector policy, and has been an expert witness and advisor in a number of court cases relating to the milk industry. David Colman has undertaken research projects and consulting contracts for various bodies, including OECD, FAO, WHO, the World Bank, ODA, and the Canadian, Malawian, and Saudi Arabian Governments. He is author of textbooks on the Principles of Agricultural Economics, on Development Economics, and of many other published works. His main areas of specialist research are in agricultural supply response, dairy sector policy (including the economics of quotas), price formation, and commodity modelling. He has a first degree in agricultural science from Wye College, and higher degrees in agricultural economics from the Universities of Illinois and Manchester.

Dr Pete Goddard

Pete Goddard is Principal Veterinary Research Officer at the Macaulay Land Use Research Institute. Prior to joining MLURI where he is responsible for the coordination of work on livestock systems, he was a lecturer in animal health at the Royal Veterinary College, London. His principal research interests are in farm animal welfare, developing new methodologies for measuring behavioural and physiological responses of animals to management practices under extensive systems.

He was educated at London University and became a member of the Royal College of Veterinary Surgeons in 1979. He was the external examiner in animal husbandry at Edinburgh University from 1995 to 1999. He is currently a Council Member for the Veterinary Deer Society and a member of the editorial advisory board of the international journal, Applied Animal Behaviour Science.

Professor Dennis Greenland

Dennis Greenland was Professor and Head of the Department of Soil Science at the University of Reading, 1969-1978, where he is a Visiting Professor in that Department. He was seconded from the University to the International Institute of Tropical Agriculture in Nigeria as Director of Research from 1974-1976, and from 1978 to 1987 he was Deputy Director General responsible for Research Programmes at the International Rice Research Institute in the Philippines. In 1987 he returned to England to become Director of the Scientific Services of CAB International, the former Commonwealth Agricultural Bureaux. He has written two books, edited seven others, and published some 150 research papers concerned with the chemistry of soil organic matter and its effects on soil properties. He was president of the British Society of Soil Science, 1976-1978, and elected as a Fellow of the Royal Society in 1994.

Dr Jeremy Greenwood

Jeremy Greenwood has been Director of the British Trust for Ornithology since 1988. The Trust is an independent charity whose purpose is to conduct surveys and research in field ornithology, using the skills of its over 11,000 members and other amateur birdwatchers combined with those of a staff of professional ornithologists, ecologists and statisticians. It is responsible for most of the monitoring of UK bird populations, not just their population sizes but also their breeding performance, survival and movements. It also conducts a range of specific research projects, many arising out of questions raised by the monitoring data. While much of the Trust's work is directed at applied issues, it does not neglect more fundamental ecological problems. Jeremy's own current interests are in the principles of applying ecological science to practical problems and in various issues in macroecology (for which the BTO's extensive and long-term data sets are particularly valuable).

Jeremy taught at the University of Dundee for twenty years prior to moving to the BTO. While there he researched the genetics and ecology of land snails, the ecology of woodland passerines, seabirds and arctic birds, and the behavioural ecology of predator/prey relationships.

He currently lives in Norfolk, where his neighbours grow a lot of sugar beet and winter cereals.

Professor Jeff Maxwell

Jeff Maxwell has been Director of the Macaulay Land Use Research Institute since 1987. He has been involved in wide ranging programmes of research and he administers and directs research programmes in integrated land use, towards sustainable development, in which the opportunities and challenges arising from new technology, including biotechnology, have been of central importance.

He was educated at Edinburgh University, was appointed Honorary Professor in Land Use Systems at the University of Aberdeen in 1987. He is a fellow of the Royal Scottish Geographical Society, of the Royal Society of Edinburgh and of the Institute of Biology, and has been a member of several advisory committees over the years. He was appointed to the Agriculture and Environment Biotechnology Commission in 2000.

Professor Hugh Pennington

Hugh Pennington was born in London and educated in Lancaster and at St Thomas's Hospital Medical School where he graduated in medicine with honours in 1962 and PhD in 1967. After house jobs and academic microbiology posts there, he spent a year at the University of Wisconsin before moving in 1969 to the Institute of Virology in Glasgow where he worked for the Medical Research Council and the University. In 1979 he was appointed to the Chair of Bacteriology at Aberdeen University. He was Dean of the Medical School from 1987-92. He chaired the Pennington Group enquiry into the 1996 *E.coli* O157 outbreak in central Scotland. In 1997 he was awarded the Caroline Walker Trust Consumer Award and was elected Fellow of the Royal Society of Edinburgh. In 1998 he became a founder Fellow of the Academy of Medical Sciences, and was awarded the John Kershaw Memorial Prize of the Royal Institute of Public Health and Hygiene and Society of Public Health. In 1999 he received an honorary D.Sc. from the University of Lancaster. Earlier this year he was appointed to the Scottish Food Advisory Committee of the Food Standards Agency.

Professor Roger Plumb

Roger Plumb took a first degree in Botany and a Ph.D in Plant Pathology. Joined Rothamsted in 1968 where he specialised in the epidemiology of virus diseases of cereals and developed an interest in viruses of tropical crops. Spent a sabbatical at Plant Research Institue, Melbourne, Australia. Became Head of Plant Pathology Department at Rothamsted in 1984, Head of Crop and Environment Protection Division in 1990, and Deputy Director IACR-Rothamsted in 1994. Retired from IACR-Rothamsted in 1999. Currently, Lawes Agricultural Trust Senior Fellow at Rothamsted, Vice-President British Society for Plant Pathology, member of the Scientific Advisory Committee of the British Beet Research Organization.

Dr Bernard Tinker

Bernard Tinker gained a 1st Class Honours degree in Chemistry in 1951 and a PhD in 1955 from Sheffield University. In 1965, he was awarded an MA and in 1983 a DSc by Oxford University. He is a Fellow of the Royal Institute of Chemistry, the Institute of Biology and the Linnean Society, an Honorary Fellow of the Royal Agricultural Society of England, and a Member of the

Norwegian Academy of Sciences. He was awarded the O.B.E in 2000, and has had awards from the Fertilizer Society and the Royal Geographical Society.

Dr Tinker has worked on many areas of soil science, particularly plant nutrition, soil/plant relations and mycorrhizal systems. His main work on field crops has been on oil palm and sugar beet. He has been President of the British Soil Science Society and a Council Member of the Society of Chemistry and Industry, of the Linnean Society and of the International Society of Soil Science.

He has worked in many places, including Nigeria and Australia, the Universities of Oxford and Leeds (Professor of Agricultural Botany), and Rothamsted Experimental Station (Deputy Director and Head of the Soils Division). He was then Director of Science in the Natural Environment Research Council of the UK until his retirement in 1992. Since then he has been active in the International Geosphere-Biosphere Programme, has chaired a number of Review Panels for CGIAR and other bodies, and has acted as a consultant for DFID and others. He has written or edited 9 books and about 180 papers.

Professor Christine Williams
Christine Willliams graduated with a BSc (Hons) Nutrition (first class) from Kings College, London. She obtained her PhD in 1978 from Guys Hospital Medical School where she studied changes in maternal adipose tissue metabolism during human pregnancy. Since then she has taught and researched extensively in many aspects of human nutrition but her major expertise is in dietary fat and heart disease. She was appointed the first Hugh Sinclair Professor of Human Nutrition at the University of Reading in 1995 and since then has established a team of 30 academics, post doctoral researchers and postgraduate students investigating mechanisms underlying relationships between diet and chronic disease. Professor Williams is member of a number of UK and European expert and advisory committees and Chairs the External Advisory Group in the Key Action area of Food, Nutrition and Health (EU Framework V). She is currently President of the Nutrition Society, is a Member of the Governing Body of the British Nutrition Foundation, the BBSRC Agri-Food Committee and the BBSRC LINK Programme Committee, Food, Eating and Health.

Acronyms

AAPS	Arable area payments
ADI	Acceptable daily intake
BAP	Biodiversity Action Plan
BTO	British Trust for Ornithology
BSE	Bovine Spongiform Encephalopathy
CAP	Common Agricultural Policy
CJD	Creutzfeldt Jakob Disease
CWS	Co-operative Wholesale Society
DETR	Department of the Environment, Transport and Regions
DNA	Deoxyribonucleic acid
EU	European Union
FBS	Farm Business Survey
FVE	Federation of Veterinarians of Europe
FWAG	Farming and Wildlife Advisory Group
FYM	Farmyard manure
GLU	Grazing livestock units
GM	Genetically modified
ha	Hectare
HACCP	Hazard Analysis and Critical Control Point system
ICM	Integrated crop management
IFOAM	International Federation of Agricultural Movements
IFS	Integrated Farming Systems
kg/ha	Kilogram per hectare
LEAF	Linking Environment and Farming
LIFE	Low Input Farming and the Environment
MAFF	Ministry of Agriculture, Fisheries and Food
MRL	Maximum residue limit
NFI	Net farm income
NFU	National Farmers' Union
NOAEL	No observable adverse effect level
OAS	Organic aid scheme
OFS	Organic farming system
ONI	Occupiers net income
pH	Measure of acidity
RSPB	Royal Society for the Protection of Birds
RSPCA	Royal Society for the Prevention of Cruelty to Animals
SA	Soil Association
SOM	Soil organic matter
TDI	Tolerable daily intake
UKROFS	UK Register of Organic Food Standards
WIRS	Welsh Institute of Rural Studies